Guideposts
DAILY PLANNER

Guideposts Daily Planner 2014

ISBN-10: 0-8249-3418-0
ISBN-13: 978-0-8249-3418-7

Published by Guideposts
16 East 34th Street
New York, New York 10016
Guideposts.org

Copyright © 2013 by Guideposts. All rights reserved.

This book, or parts thereof, may not be reproduced, stored in a retrieval system, or transmitted in any form or by any means, electronic, mechanical, photocopying, recording or otherwise, without the written permission of the publisher.

Distributed by Ideals Publications, a Guideposts company
2630 Elm Hill Pike, Suite 100
Nashville, TN 37214

Guideposts, Ideals and *Guideposts Daily Planner* are registered trademarks of Guideposts.

Acknowledgments

Every attempt has been made to credit the sources of copyrighted material used in this book. If any such acknowledgment has been inadvertently omitted or miscredited, receipt of such information would be appreciated.

Scripture quotations marked (AMP) are from the *Amplified Bible*. Copyright © 1954, 1958, 1962, 1964, 1965, 1987 by the Lockman Foundation.

Scripture quotations marked (CEB) are taken from the *Common English Bible*. Copyright © 2011 by Common English Bible.

Scripture quotations marked (CEV) are taken from *Holy Bible: Contemporary English Version*. Copyright © 1995 American Bible Society.

Scripture quotations marked (CJB) are taken from *Complete Jewish Bible*. Copyright © 1998 by David H. Stern. All rights reserved.

Scripture quotations marked (ESV) are taken from the *Holy Bible, English Standard Version*, copyright © 2001 by Crossway Bibles, a division of Good News Publishers. Used by permission. All rights reserved.

Scripture quotations marked (GNB) are taken from the *Good News Bible Today's English Version*. Copyright © 1992 by the American Bible Society.

Scripture quotations marked (KJV) are taken from *The King James Version of the Bible*.

Scripture quotations marked (MSG) are taken from *The Message*. Copyright © 1993, 1994, 1995, 1996, 2000, 2001, 2002 by Eugene H. Peterson.

Scripture quotations marked (NAS) are taken from the *New American Standard Bible*, copyright © 1960, 1962, 1963, 1968, 1971, 1972, 1973, 1975, 1977, 1995 by the Lockman Foundation. Used by permission.

Scripture quotations marked (NIV) are taken from *The Holy Bible, New International Version*. Copyright © 1973, 1978, 1984, 2011 by Biblica.

Scripture quotations marked (NKJV) are taken from *The Holy Bible, New King James Version*. Copyright © 1997, 1990, 1985, 1983 by Thomas Nelson, Inc.

Scripture quotations marked (NLT) are from the *Holy Bible, New Living Translation*. Copyright© 1996, 2004, 2007 by Tyndale House Foundation. Used by permission of Tyndale House Publishers Inc., Carol Stream, Illinois 60188. All rights reserved.

Scripture quotations marked (NRSV) are taken from the *New Revised Standard Version Bible*. Copyright © 1989 by the Division of Christian Education of the National Council of the Churches of Christ in the United States of America. Used by permission. All rights reserved.

Scripture quotations marked (RSV) are taken from the *Revised Standard Version of the Bible*. Copyright © 1946, 1952, 1971 by Division of Christian Education of the National Council of Churches of Christ in the United States of America. Used by permission.

Scripture quotations marked (TIB) are taken from *The Inclusive Bible: The First Egalitarian Translation*. Copyright © 2007 by Priests for Equality. All rights reserved.

Scripture quotations marked (TLB) are taken from *The Living Bible*. Copyright © 1971 by Tyndale House Publishers, Wheaton, Illinois 60187. All rights reserved.

Scripture quotations marked (TNIV) are taken from *Holy Bible, Today's New International Version*. Copyright © 2001, 2005 by Biblica. All rights reserved worldwide.

Cover and interior design and typesetting by Müllerhaus
Cover photo by Corbis

Printed and bound in the United States of America
10 9 8 7 6 5 4 3 2 1

2014

Guideposts
DAILY PLANNER

Guideposts
New York

Now faith is the substance of things hoped for, the evidence of things not seen. —HEBREWS 11:1 (KJV)

PRAYER FOR THE MONTH OF NEW BEGINNINGS

Abba, at midnight, when the old year dies
And the new comes bounding in,
I like to be away from the clatter of celebration,
In the country, outdoors.
For I have found that it is in nature,
In Your real world, that I touch reassurance.
When I stand outside, close to the earth,
   in the good cold air,
I draw strength from knowing
That in the next twelve months
   the snows will go, the buds will burst
   the heat will rise, the leaves will fly,
That all these things will happen
   according to Your schedule and in
   your time;
That there is order in Your universe,
And that I am part of it.

JANUARY 2014

A LIVING PARABLE FOR JANUARY
HOPE by Van Varner

I went on a writing assignment to Pennsylvania, where a week before a flash flood had roared down from the Pocono Mountains. *What,* I wondered, *could be redeeming about the mud and destruction waiting there?*

Well, I found it through a group who'd come from a Mennonite church two hours away. Farmers, lawyers and tradesmen—they brought their shovels and wheelbarrows and pitched in to dig the town out.

A pregnant woman was forced to flee in waist-high water—a baby held over her head, another child clutching tightly to her neck. They reached safety, but it was two days before the frantic husband found them. Everything in their house was ruined, covered with thick mud.

"My house is everything I own," he told me. "When I came back, I just sat outside, paralyzed. I'd lost hope. Then the Mennonites started to work on *my* place."

I saw then what those good Mennonites were actually contributing: hope. Hope cuts a path through the darkness. Like faith, it is an intangible that makes life livable and rich.

This year, let's all hold fast to hope. And like those Mennonite shovelers, let's find opportunities to give it away to others.

JANUARY 2014

SUNDAY	MONDAY	TUESDAY	WEDNESDAY	THURSDAY	FRIDAY	SATURDAY
			1 NEW YEAR'S DAY	2	3	4
5	6	7	8	9	10	11
12	13	14	15	16	17	18
19	20 MARTIN LUTHER KING JR. DAY	21	22	23	24	25
26	27	28	29	30	31	

NOTES

DECEMBER 2013

S	M	T	W	T	F	S
1	2	3	4	5	6	7
8	9	10	11	12	13	14
15	16	17	18	19	20	21
22	23	24	25	26	27	28
29	30	31				

FEBRUARY

S	M	T	W	T	F	S
						1
2	3	4	5	6	7	8
9	10	11	12	13	14	15
16	17	18	19	20	21	22
23	24	25	26	27	28	

GUIDEPOSTS DAILY PLANNER

OUR PRAYER: *Dear God, show me how I can welcome the visitor You send to my door.*

JANUARY

DECEMBER 2013

29
SUNDAY

"See to it that you never despise one of these little ones, for I swear that their angels in heaven are continually in the presence of my Abba God." –Matthew 18:10 (TIB)

30
MONDAY

"Peace I leave with you, My peace I give to you; not as the world gives do I give to you. Let not your heart be troubled , neither let it be afraid." John 14:27 (NKJV)

31
TUESDAY

NEW YEAR'S EVE

Ascribe to the Lord the glory due his name; bring an offering and come before him. Worship the Lord in the splendor of his holiness. —1 Chronicles 16:29 (TNIV)

JANUARY

S	M	T	W	T	F	S
			1	2	3	4
5	6	7	8	9	10	11
12	13	14	15	16	17	18
19	20	21	22	23	24	25
26	27	28	29	30	31	

PRAYER REQUESTS _____

_____

_____

_____

_____

JANUARY 2014

❧ JANUARY 2014 ❧

JANUARY

1
WEDNESDAY

NEW YEAR'S
DAY

Use hospitality one to another.... —1 Peter 4:9 (KJV)

2
THURSDAY

This is the day which the Lord hath made; we will rejoice and be glad in it.
—Psalm 118: 24 (KJV)

3
FRIDAY

Let us not lose heart in doing good, for in due time we will reap if we do not grow weary.
—Galatians 6:9 (NAS)

4
SATURDAY

Be joyful in hope, patient in affliction, faithful in prayer. Share with the Lord's people
who are in need.... —Romans 12:12–13 (NIV)

GUIDEPOSTS DAILY PLANNER

OUR PRAYER: *Thank You, God, for friendship in all its blessed forms.*

JANUARY

5
SUNDAY

For by grace you have been saved through faith, and that not of yourselves; it is the gift of God. —Ephesians 2:8 (NKJV)

6
MONDAY

When I consider thy heavens, the work of thy fingers, the moon and the stars, which thou hast ordained; What is man, that thou art mindful of him? —Psalm 8:3–4 (KJV)

7
TUESDAY

Who hopes for what they already have? But if we hope for what we do not yet have, we wait for it patiently. —Romans 8: 24–25 (NIV)

JANUARY

S	M	T	W	T	F	S
			1	2	3	4
5	6	7	8	9	10	11
12	13	14	15	16	17	18
19	20	21	22	23	24	25
26	27	28	29	30	31	

PRAYER REQUESTS _____

_____

_____

_____

_____

JANUARY 2014

❖ JANUARY 2014 ❖

JANUARY

8
WEDNESDAY

Not only so, but we also glory in our sufferings, because we know that suffering produces perseverance; perseverance, character; and character, hope. —Romans 5:3–4 (NIV)

9
THURSDAY

I urge, then, first of all, that petitions, prayers, intercession and thanksgiving be made for all people. —1 Timothy 2:1 (NIV)

10
FRIDAY

Place these words on your hearts. Get them deep inside you.... —Deuteronomy 11:18 (MSG)

11
SATURDAY

And the streets of the city shall be full of boys and girls playing in the streets thereof. —Zechariah 8:5 (KJV)

GUIDEPOSTS DAILY PLANNER

OUR PRAYER: *Dear God, help me claim the happy moments that come my way this week.*

JANUARY

12
SUNDAY

The Lord has done it this very day; let us rejoice today and be glad. —Psalm 118:24 (NIV)

13
MONDAY

He is before all things, and in him all things hold together. —Colossians 1:17 (NIV)

14
TUESDAY

I instruct you in the way of wisdom and lead you along straight paths. —Proverbs 4:11 (NIV)

JANUARY

S	M	T	W	T	F	S
			1	2	3	4
5	6	7	8	9	10	11
12	13	14	15	16	17	18
19	20	21	22	23	24	25
26	27	28	29	30	31	

PRAYER REQUESTS _____

_____

_____

_____

_____

JANUARY 2014

❧ JANUARY 2014 ❧

JANUARY

15
WEDNESDAY

"For I know the plans that I have for you," declares the Lord, "plans to give you a future and a hope." —Jeremiah 29:11 (NAS)

16
THURSDAY

Take delight in the Lord, and he will give you the desires of your heart. —Psalm 37:4 (NIV)

17
FRIDAY

"I will bring peace, peace to those far and near".... —Isaiah 57:19 (TIB)

18
SATURDAY

Giving thanks always for all things.... —Ephesians 5:20 (KJV)

GUIDEPOSTS DAILY PLANNER

OUR PRAYER: *Dear God, thank You so much for being the real leader of our faith community.*

JANUARY

19
SUNDAY

Moses was...more humble than anyone else on the face of the earth. —Numbers 12:3 (NIV)

20
MONDAY

MARTIN LUTHER
KING JR. DAY

The Lord gives sight to the blind.... —Psalm 146:8 (NIV)

21
TUESDAY

"For I am the Lord your God who takes hold of your right hand and says to you,
Do not fear; I will help you." —Isaiah 41:13 (NIV)

JANUARY

S	M	T	W	T	F	S
			1	2	3	4
5	6	7	8	9	10	11
12	13	14	15	16	17	18
19	20	21	22	23	24	25
26	27	28	29	30	31	

PRAYER REQUESTS

JANUARY 2014

❋ JANUARY 2014 ❋

JANUARY

22
WEDNESDAY

Always try to do good to each other and to everyone else. —1 Thessalonians 5:15 (TLB)

23
THURSDAY

Do your best to improve your faith. You can do this by adding goodness, understanding, self-control, patience, devotion to God, concern for others, and love. —2 Peter 1:5–7 (CEV)

24
FRIDAY

"Therefore a man shall leave his father and mother and hold fast to his wife, and the two shall become one flesh." This mystery is profound.... —Ephesians 5:31–32 (ESV)

25
SATURDAY

God setteth the solitary in families.... —Psalm 68:6 (KJV)

GUIDEPOSTS DAILY PLANNER

OUR PRAYER: *Dear God, thank You for the day of rest— just what I need to relax and feel blessed.*

JANUARY

26 SUNDAY

"Six days you shall labor and do all your work, but the seventh day is a Sabbath to the Lord your God. On it you shall not do any work...." —Deuteronomy 5:13–14 (NIV)

27 MONDAY

"You are the salt of the earth...." —Matthew 5:13 (NRSV)

28 TUESDAY

Finally, all of you, have unity of mind, sympathy, brotherly love, a tender heart, and a humble mind. —1 Peter 3:8 (ESV)

JANUARY

S	M	T	W	T	F	S
			1	2	3	4
5	6	7	8	9	10	11
12	13	14	15	16	17	18
19	20	21	22	23	24	25
26	27	28	29	30	31	

PRAYER REQUESTS _____

JANUARY 2014

❧ JANUARY 2014 ❧

JANUARY

29
WEDNESDAY

Dear friends, let us love one another, for love comes from God. Everyone who loves has been born of God and knows God. —1 John 4:7 (NIV)

30
THURSDAY

If my people…shall humble themselves, and pray…then will I…forgive their sin.… —2 Chronicles 7:14 (KJV)

31
FRIDAY

"It laughs at fear, afraid of nothing; it does not shy away from the sword." —Job 39:22 (NIV)

FEBRUARY

1
SATURDAY

Moreover, He said to me, "Son of man, take into your heart all My words which I will speak to you and listen closely." —Ezekiel 3:10 (NAS)

GUIDEPOSTS DAILY PLANNER

As he thinketh in his heart, so is he.... —PROVERBS 23:7 (KJV)

PRAYER FOR THE MONTH OF SILENT SLUMBER

Oh, God,
Silent are Your woods now where the snows lie deep.
The days are rimed with frost, the nights are long.
The world's asleep, dreaming of sunshine,
Waiting for spring to come with its warm green kiss
That wakens everything.
Sometimes my soul seems like the woods,
Silent, motionless and chill, waiting for a signal,
Unable to make it happen, but knowing it will come.
Speak to my waiting soul, God,
Call me into the warmth of Your presence, and Your love.

FEBRUARY 2014

A LIVING PARABLE FOR FEBRUARY
CHOOSE HAPPINESS
by Van Varner

I had gone to Dr. Norman Vincent Peale's office for an interview that would determine whether I was to be hired at Guideposts. It seemed to be going well until Dr. Peale asked, "Tell me, are you a happy man?"

The question caught me off guard. "Well, yes," I replied, "I guess I'd have to say that I am."

This news seemed to please him. "Good," he said. "Of course, we all have two choices, don't we? We can choose to be happy or we can choose to be unhappy."

"Yes," I said, but my reply didn't ooze with conviction. Frankly, I wasn't altogether sure what the good doctor was getting at. Then the telephone rang, and we never got back to the subject.

I did get the job though, and years later I know exactly what Dr. Peale was saying. Our conscious decision to be happy creates a climate where happiness can take root and grow, for attitudes shape the direction of our lives.

Most of us have a long list of reasons for happiness than we are inclined to admit. We have people to love and people who love us. We have our integrity. We live in a great and caring country. And just in case those are not enough, we have the breath of life and a God Who loves us.

❧ FEBRUARY 2014 ❧

SUNDAY	MONDAY	TUESDAY	WEDNESDAY	THURSDAY	FRIDAY	SATURDAY
						1
2	3	4	5	8	7	8
9	10	11	12 ABRAHAM LINCOLN'S BIRTHDAY	13	14 VALENTINE'S DAY	15
16	17 PRESIDENTS' DAY	18	19	20	21	22 GEORGE WASHINGTON'S BIRTHDAY
23	24	25	26	27	28	

NOTES

JANUARY

S	M	T	W	T	F	S
			1	2	3	4
5	6	7	8	9	10	11
12	13	14	15	16	17	18
19	20	21	22	23	24	25
26	27	28	29	30	31	

MARCH

S	M	T	W	T	F	S
						1
2	3	4	5	6	7	8
9	10	11	12	13	14	15
16	17	18	19	20	21	22
23/30	24/31	25	26	27	28	29

GUIDEPOSTS DAILY PLANNER

OUR PRAYER: *God, when my days are glum, remind me to ask You to brighten them.*

FEBRUARY

2
SUNDAY

The Lord is good to all: and his tender mercies are over all his works. —Psalm 145:9 (KJV)

3
MONDAY

Therefore we are always confident and know that as long as we are at home in the body we are away from the Lord. For we live by faith, not by sight. —2 Corinthians 5: 6–7 (NIV)

4
TUESDAY

The Lord my God lightens my darkness. —Psalm 18:28 (RSV)

FEBRUARY

S	M	T	W	T	F	S
						1
2	3	4	5	6	7	8
9	10	11	12	13	14	15
16	17	18	19	20	21	22
23	24	25	26	27	28	

PRAYER REQUESTS _____

FEBRUARY 2014

➤ FEBRUARY 2014 ◄

5
WEDNESDAY

Your heavenly Father knoweth that ye have need of all these things. —Matthew 6:32 (KJV)

6
THURSDAY

"I will change my expression, and smile." —Job 9:27 (NIV)

7
FRIDAY

"I will not let you go, unless you bless me." —Genesis 32:26 (RSV)

8
SATURDAY

And He will be the stability of your times.... —Isaiah 33:6 (NAS)

FEBRUARY

OUR PRAYER: *Creator, I pray for the day when all of us grasp the unlimited reservoir of Your love and can finally see its regenerating power.*

FEBRUARY

9
SUNDAY

Mercy and truth are met together; righteousness and peace have kissed each other. —Psalm 85:10 (KJV)

10
MONDAY

So foolish was I; and ignorant…. —Psalm 73:22 (KJV)

11
TUESDAY

"For my thoughts are not your thoughts, neither are your ways my ways," declares the Lord. —Isaiah 55:8 (NIV)

FEBRUARY

S	M	T	W	T	F	S
						1
2	3	4	5	6	7	8
9	10	11	12	13	14	15
16	17	18	19	20	21	22
23	24	25	26	27	28	

PRAYER REQUESTS _____

_____

_____

_____

_____

FEBRUARY 2014

❋ FEBRUARY 2014 ❋

12
WEDNESDAY

ABRAHAM
LINCOLN'S
BIRTHDAY

This service that you perform is not only supplying the needs of the Lord's people but is also overflowing in many expressions of thanks to God. —2 Corinthians 9:12 (NIV)

13
THURSDAY

"Don't recite the same prayer over and over as the heathen do, who think prayers are answered only by repeating them again and again. —Matthew 6:7-8 (TLB)

14
FRIDAY

VALENTINE'S
DAY

Be completely humble and gentle; be patient, bearing with one another in love. —Ephesians 4:2 (NIV)

15
SATURDAY

Trust in the Lord with all your heart, and do not lean on your own understanding. In all your ways acknowledge Him, and He will make straight your paths. —Proverbs 3: 5–6 (ESV)

OUR PRAYER: *God, show me ways to give tangible thanks to those who have been kind to me.*

FEBRUARY

16
SUNDAY

In this vision he saw an angel of God coming toward him.... —Acts 10:3 (TLB)

17
MONDAY

"I truly understand that God shows no partiality, but in every nation anyone who fears him and does what is right is acceptable to him." —Acts 10:34–35 (NRSV)

18
TUESDAY

PRESIDENTS'
DAY

"Love your enemies! Do good to them. Lend to them without expecting to be repaid.... You will truly be acting as children of the Most High...." —Luke 6:35 (NLT)

FEBRUARY

S	M	T	W	T	F	S
						1
2	3	4	5	6	7	8
9	10	11	12	13	14	15
16	17	18	19	20	21	22
23	24	25	26	27	28	

PRAYER REQUESTS _____

FEBRUARY 2014

✦ FEBRUARY 2014 ✦

FEBRUARY

19
WEDNESDAY

"Can you fathom the mysteries of God? Can you probe the limits of the Almighty?"
—Job 11:7 (NIV)

20
THURSDAY

Behold, this is the joy of his way, and out of the earth shall others grow. —Job 8:19 (KJV)

21
FRIDAY

Be ye kind one to another, tenderhearted…. —Ephesians 4:32 (ASV)

22
SATURDAY

GEORGE
WASHINGTON'S
BIRTHDAY

Lord my God, I called to you for help and you healed me. —Psalm 30:2 (NIV)

GUIDEPOSTS DAILY PLANNER

OUR PRAYER: *Holy Spirit, speak the words I cannot utter.*

FEBRUARY

23
SUNDAY

We do not know what we ought to pray for, but the Spirit himself intercedes for us through wordless groans. —Romans 8:26 (NIV)

24
MONDAY

Be still before the Lord and wait patiently for him.... —Psalm 37:7 (NIV)

25
TUESDAY

It is good for people to eat, drink, and enjoy their work.... —Ecclesiastes 5:18 (NLT)

FEBRUARY

S	M	T	W	T	F	S
						1
2	3	4	5	6	7	8
9	10	11	12	13	14	15
16	17	18	19	20	21	22
23	24	25	26	27	28	

PRAYER REQUESTS _____

FEBRUARY 2014

❧ FEBRUARY 2014 ❧

FEBRUARY

26
WEDNESDAY

Love one another...as members of one family.... —Romans 12:10 (AMP)

27
THURSDAY

Love never fails.... —1 Corinthians 13:8 (NKJV)

28
FRIDAY

Our Father which art in heaven, Hallowed be thy name. Thy kingdom come....
—Matthew 6:9–10 (KJV)

MARCH

1
SATURDAY

Rejoice always, pray continually, give thanks in all circumstances; for this is God's will for you in Christ Jesus. —1 Thessalonians 5:16–18 (NIV)

GUIDEPOSTS DAILY PLANNER

Commit thy way unto the Lord, trust also in him; and he shall bring it to pass. —PSALM 37:5 (KJV)

PRAYER FOR THE MONTH OF CLEANSING WINDS

God, this is the month
When You use the wind as a cleaning rag
To polish the dappled sky,
And sometimes when You do,
High up there against the burnished blue,
The young-in-heart fly kites.
I love to watch them dip and soar,
Colorful as confetti, saucy as swallows,
Climbing, swaying, tugging, darting,
Praising the unseen force that holds them up.
And I—oh, I'm like them too, God,
I must have Your sustaining presence
Under me if I'm to soar
Above the muddy fields and muddled hours.
Breathe on me, God. Hold me up high,
Not just today—every day.

A LIVING PARABLE FOR MARCH
SURRENDER by Van Varner

Catherine Marshall was a woman of luminous faith and a practical Christian who wrote from her own experience. The foundation of her faith, the touchstone she always kept at hand, was the soul-deep change she underwent many years before she had published a single word.

Catherine was a young wife and mother—married to the much-admired pastor Peter Marshall—when she fell ill with what she always described as "a widespread lung infection." She never used the word *tuberculosis*. She languished in bed for months, and the months turned into years. As her body grew thinner so did her spirit. Then came a day of decision. Catherine stopped struggling. She stopped beseeching God to do as *she* asked and let God do as God desired.

"I gave God a blank check," she told me. Catherine surrendered her vanity, willfulness, sins, worries, happiness and, yes, her life. From that point on, she began to recover.

"The crisis of self-surrender"—that's what the philosopher William James called it. He described it as the vital turning point of religious life. It was for Catherine Marshall the surest step toward God that a human being can take.

MARCH 2014

SUNDAY	MONDAY	TUESDAY	WEDNESDAY	THURSDAY	FRIDAY	SATURDAY
						1
2	3	4	5 ASH WEDNESDAY	8	7	8
9 DAYLIGHT SAVING TIME BEGINS	10	11	12	13	14	15
16	17 ST. PATRICK'S DAY	18	19	20 SPRING BEGINS	21	22
23 30	24 31	25	26	27	28	29

NOTES

FEBRUARY

S	M	T	W	T	F	S
						1
2	3	4	5	6	7	8
9	10	11	12	13	14	15
16	17	18	19	20	21	22
23	24	25	26	27	28	

APRIL

S	M	T	W	T	F	S
		1	2	3	4	5
6	7	8	9	10	11	12
13	14	15	16	17	18	19
20	21	22	23	24	25	26
27	28	29	30			

GUIDEPOSTS DAILY PLANNER

OUR PRAYER: *Abba, keep my attention where it really belongs—on You.*

MARCH

2
SUNDAY

If any man among you seem to be religious, and bridleth not his tongue, but deceiveth his own heart, this man's religion is vain. —James 1:26 (KJV)

3
MONDAY

...Who through faith...whose weakness was turned to strength.... —Hebrews 11:33-34 (NIV)

4
TUESDAY

But as for me, it is good to be near God.... —Psalm 73:28 (NIV)

MARCH

S	M	T	W	T	F	S
						1
2	3	4	5	6	7	8
9	10	11	12	13	14	15
16	17	18	19	20	21	22
23/30	24/31	25	26	27	28	29

PRAYER REQUESTS _____

_____

_____

_____

_____

MARCH 2014

❧ MARCH 2014 ❧

5
WEDNESDAY

ASH
WEDNESDAY

Let us draw near with a true heart in full assurance of faith, having our hearts sprinkled from an evil conscience, and our bodies washed with pure water. —Hebrews 10:22 (KJV)

6
THURSDAY

Therefore, if anyone is in Christ, the new creation has come: The old has gone, the new is here! —2 Corinthians 5:17 (NIV)

7
FRIDAY

"Stop judging by mere appearances, but instead judge correctly." —John 7:24 (NIV)

8
SATURDAY

Gracious words are like a honeycomb, sweetness to the soul.... —Proverbs 16:24 (ESV)

MARCH

GUIDEPOSTS DAILY PLANNER

OUR PRAYER: *Dear God, may I always be mindful of the beauty in every season You have placed beneath my feet.*

MARCH

9
SUNDAY

DAYLIGHT
SAVING TIME
BEGINS

"As long as the earth endures, seedtime and harvest, cold and heat, summer and winter, day and night will never cease." —Genesis 8:22 (NIV)

10
MONDAY

O that today you would hearken to his voice! —Psalm 95:7 (RSV)

11
TUESDAY

"For the mouth speaks what the heart is full of." —Luke 6:45 (NIV)

MARCH

S	M	T	W	T	F	S
						1
2	3	4	5	6	7	8
9	10	11	12	13	14	15
16	17	18	19	20	21	22
23/30	24/31	25	26	27	28	29

PRAYER REQUESTS _____

_____

_____

_____

_____

MARCH 2014

❧ MARCH 2014 ❧

MARCH

12
WEDNESDAY

Be ye strong therefore, and let not your hands be weak: for your work shall be rewarded. —2 Chronicles 15:7 (KJV)

13
THURSDAY

Blessed are they which do hunger and thirst after righteousness: for they shall be filled. —Matthew 5:6 (KJV)

14
FRIDAY

Since God chose you...you must clothe yourselves with tenderhearted mercy.... —Colossians 3:12 (NLT)

15
SATURDAY

Satisfy us in the morning with your unfailing love, that we may sing for joy and be glad all our days. —Psalm 90:14 (NIV)

GUIDEPOSTS DAILY PLANNER

OUR PRAYER: *God, turn my eyes to where You are shining, and I will have found my way.*

MARCH

16
SUNDAY

Moses built an altar and named it The Lord is My Banner. —Exodus 17:15 (NAS)

17
MONDAY

ST. PATRICK'S
DAY

Let the nations be glad and sing for joy.... —Psalm 67:4 (KJV)

18
TUESDAY

"You're blessed when you're at the end of your rope. With less of you there is more of God and his rule." —Matthew 5:3 (MSG)

MARCH

S	M	T	W	T	F	S
						1
2	3	4	5	6	7	8
9	10	11	12	13	14	15
16	17	18	19	20	21	22
23/30	24/31	25	26	27	28	29

PRAYER REQUESTS _____

MARCH 2014

✦ MARCH 2014 ✦

19
WEDNESDAY

"It will produce branches and bear fruit and become a splendid cedar...." —Ezekiel 17:23 (NIV)

20
THURSDAY

SPRING
BEGINS

"And remember, I am with you always...." —Matthew 28:20 (NRSV)

21
FRIDAY

He heals the brokenhearted and binds up their wounds. —Psalm 147:3 (NIV)

22
SATURDAY

O Lord, you have freed me from my bonds and I will serve you forever. —Psalm 116:16 (TLB)

MARCH

GUIDEPOSTS DAILY PLANNER

OUR PRAYER: *Today's a brand-new era, God. Help me to really look forward to it. Amen.*

MARCH

23
SUNDAY

...Forgetting those things which are behind and reaching forward to those things which are ahead. —Philippians 3:13 (NKJV)

24
MONDAY

"I was hungry and you gave me food...." —Matthew 25:35 (RSV)

25
TUESDAY

Joy cometh in the morning. —Psalm 30:5 (KJV)

MARCH

S	M	T	W	T	F	S
						1
2	3	4	5	6	7	8
9	10	11	12	13	14	15
16	17	18	19	20	21	22
23/30	24/31	25	26	27	28	29

PRAYER REQUESTS _____

_____

_____

_____

_____

MARCH 2014

❧ MARCH 2014 ❧

26 WEDNESDAY

He gives food to every creature. His love endures forever. —Psalm 136:25 (NIV)

27 THURSDAY

All my longings lie open before you, Lord; my sighing is not hidden from you.
—Psalm 38:9 (NIV)

28 FRIDAY

"Therefore do not worry about tomorrow, for tomorrow will worry about itself.
Each day has enough trouble of its own." —Matthew 6:34 (NIV)

29 SATURDAY

My strength and power are made perfect—fulfilled and completed and show
themselves most effective—in [your] weakness.... —2 Corinthians 12:9 (AMP)

MARCH

GUIDEPOSTS DAILY PLANNER

Thy faith hath made thee whole.... —MATTHEW 9:22 (KJV)

PRAYER FOR THE MONTH OF PROMISE

God,
One poet has called this the cruelest month
Because with spring there is birth,
And with birth there is pain.
But I don't think there really is
A cruel month in Your kindom.
I'm not a poet, God, but I love April
Because it makes a promise and then delivers.
The promise is the first warm whiff
Of Your good earth.
The gift is the profusion
Of blooms that makes my drab world sing.
A gift so fresh and new, each year that it seems
As if it were being given for the first time.

APRIL 2014

A LIVING PARABLE FOR APRIL
SERVING OTHERS
by Van Varner

When I met Grace Oursler, the widow of the famed writer-editor Fulton Oursler, she was engaged in a long war with ill health. And what a glorious battle that was, for Grace was a courageous fighter.

"I've often wondered," she said, "why my prayers for others get such prompt attention, while personal requests seem to go begging." She was not complaining, just making an observation. Then she added, "I've concluded God has some special use for my illness."

I think she knew what that use was, for on another occasion she talked about the shrine at Lourdes in France where so many remarkable healings had been recorded. "When patients arrive there, they don't just lie around. They're expected to work." Then Grace explained how the sick are required to tend to the needs of their fellow sufferers and to pray for both the sick and the well.

"The strange phenomenon of Lourdes," Grace said, "is how quickly the sick forget about themselves. When that happens, their prayers are like dynamite! That's when many of the healings happen."

Grace Oursler knew that God answers prayer and that the beautiful mystery is God does it in God's own way. For she was surely healed. By serving people, she was made spiritually whole. And that is the greatest healing of all.

❧ APRIL 2014 ❧

SUNDAY	MONDAY	TUESDAY	WEDNESDAY	THURSDAY	FRIDAY	SATURDAY
		1	2	3	4	5
6	7	8	9	10	11	12
13 PALM SUNDAY	14	15 PASSOVER	16	17 MAUNDY THURSDAY	18 GUIDEPOSTS GOOD FRIDAY DAY OF PRAYER	19
20 EASTER	21	22 EARTH DAY	23	24	25	26
27	28	29	30			

NOTES

MARCH

S	M	T	W	T	F	S
						1
2	3	4	5	6	7	8
9	10	11	12	13	14	15
16	17	18	19	20	21	22
23/30	24/31	25	26	27	28	29

MAY

S	M	T	W	T	F	S
				1	2	3
4	5	6	7	8	9	10
11	12	13	14	15	16	17
18	19	20	21	22	23	24
25	26	27	28	29	30	31

GUIDEPOSTS DAILY PLANNER

OUR PRAYER: *Guide my life, God, by Your Words;*
that in hearing them, I may live according to Your wishes.

APRIL

MARCH

30
SUNDAY

Great are the works of the Lord; they are pondered by all who delight in them. —Psalm 111:2 (NIV)

31
MONDAY

He leadeth me beside the still waters. He restoreth my soul.... —Psalm 23:2–3 (KJV)

APRIL

1
TUESDAY

In your light we see light. —Psalm 36:9 (NIV)

APRIL

S	M	T	W	T	F	S
		1	2	3	4	5
6	7	8	9	10	11	12
13	14	15	16	17	18	19
20	21	22	23	24	25	26
27	28	29	30			

PRAYER REQUESTS

APRIL 2014

❧ APRIL 2014 ❧

2 WEDNESDAY

Remember now your Creator in the days of your youth, before the difficult days come, and the years dra w near when you say, "I have no pleasure in them." —Ecclesiastes 12:1 (NKJV)

3 THURSDAY

The Lord bless you and keep you; the Lord make his face to shine upon you, and be gracious to you. —Numbers 6:24–25 (NRSV)

4 FRIDAY

"God has dealt graciously with me and…I have plenty." —Genesis 33:11 (NAS)

5 SATURDAY

But everything comes from God. —1 Corinthians 11:12 (NIV)

APRIL

GUIDEPOSTS DAILY PLANNER

OUR PRAYER: *Jesus, thank You for all You give me—*
over and above grace—that I neither earn nor deserve.

6
SUNDAY

...That God will open up to us a door for the word, so that we may speak forth the mystery of Christ.... —Colossians 4:3 (NAS)

7
MONDAY

"Be strong and courageous. Do not be afraid; do not be discouraged, for the Lord your God will be with you wherever you go." —Joshua 1:9 (NIV)

8
TUESDAY

Trust in the Lord with all your heart and lean not on your own understanding. —Proverbs 3:5 (NIV)

APRIL

APRIL

S	M	T	W	T	F	S
		1	2	3	4	5
6	7	8	9	10	11	12
13	14	15	16	17	18	19
20	21	22	23	24	25	26
27	28	29	30			

PRAYER REQUESTS

APRIL 2014

❋ APRIL 2014 ❋

9 WEDNESDAY
Christ is...in all. —Colossians 3:11 (KJV)

10 THURSDAY
I lay down My life for the sheep. —John 10:15 (NAS)

11 FRIDAY
The Lord is my rock.... —Psalm 18:2 (KJV)

12 SATURDAY
"For I am the Lord your God who takes hold of your right hand and says to you, Do not fear; I will help you." —Isaiah 41:13 (NIV)

APRIL

GUIDEPOSTS DAILY PLANNER

OUR PRAYER: *Dear God, we often praise You one day, then betray You the next. Let us overcome our fickle nature and be faithful companions to You and our brothers and sisters.*

APRIL

13
SUNDAY
PALM SUNDAY

And the crowds that went before him and that followed him shouted, "Hosanna to the Son of David!..." —Matthew 21:8–9 (RSV)

14
MONDAY

"Then shall the maidens rejoice in the dance, and the young men and the old shall be merry. I will turn their mourning into joy...." —Jeremiah 31:13 (RSV)

15
TUESDAY
PASSOVER

And being in an agony he prayed more earnestly: and his sweat was as it were great drops of blood falling down to the ground. —Luke 22:44 (KJV)

APRIL

S	M	T	W	T	F	S
		1	2	3	4	5
6	7	8	9	10	11	12
13	14	15	16	17	18	19
20	21	22	23	24	25	26
27	28	29	30			

PRAYER REQUESTS

APRIL 2014

❧ APRIL 2014 ❧

16
WEDNESDAY

And as they came out, they found a man of Cyrene, Simon by name: him they compelled to bear his cross. —Matthew 27:32 (KJV)

17
THURSDAY

MAUNDY
THURSDAY

They went to a place which was called Gethsemane; and he said to his disciples, "Sit here, while I pray." —Mark 14:32 (RSV)

18
FRIDAY

GUIDEPOSTS
GOOD FRIDAY
DAY OF PRAYER

There followed him a great company…of women, which also bewailed and lamented him. But Jesus turning unto them said, Daughters of Jerusalem, weep not for me.… —Luke 23:27–28 (KJV)

19
SATURDAY

May God who gives patience…and encouragement help you to live in complete harmony with each other.… —Romans 15:5 (TLB)

APRIL

GUIDEPOSTS DAILY PLANNER

OUR PRAYER: *Dear God, help rid me of my selfish ego. Granted, ego is easy and forgiveness is difficult . . . but today, of all days, I'm willing to try the hard way.*

20 SUNDAY
EASTER

...The children of God, being the children of the resurrection.... For he is not a God of the dead, but of the living: for all live unto him. —Luke 20:36 –38 (KJV)

21 MONDAY

Blessed are those who trust in the Lord.... —Jeremiah 17:7 (NRSV)

22 TUESDAY
EARTH DAY

O Lord, how many are Your works! In wisdom You have made them all.... —Psalm 104:24 (NAS)

APRIL

S	M	T	W	T	F	S
		1	2	3	4	5
6	7	8	9	10	11	12
13	14	15	16	17	18	19
20	21	22	23	24	25	26
27	28	29	30			

PRAYER REQUESTS _____

APRIL 2014

❧ APRIL 2014 ❧

23 WEDNESDAY

"You did not choose me, but I chose you and appointed you so that you might go and bear fruit ...that will last...." —John 15:16 (NIV)

24 THURSDAY

No one can bring them back to life to enjoy what will be in the future, so let them enjoy it now. —Ecclesiastes 3:22 (TLB)

25 FRIDAY

"Let your light shine before others, so that they may see your good works and give glory to your Father in heaven." —Matthew 5:16 (NRSV)

26 SATURDAY

"I have not stopped giving thanks for you, remembering you in my prayers." —Ephesians 1:16 (NIV)

APRIL

GUIDEPOSTS DAILY PLANNER

OUR PRAYER: *God, thank You for reminding me that the best place for any church is on Your rock, not my pedestal. Amen.*

APRIL

27 SUNDAY

But he said to me, "My grace is sufficient for you, for my power is made perfect in weakness".... —2 Corinthians 12:9 (NIV)

28 MONDAY

For you make me glad by your deeds, Lord; I sing for joy at what your hands have done. —Psalm 92:4 (NIV)

29 TUESDAY

The disciples were together, with the doors locked for fear.... —John 20:19 (NIV)

APRIL

S	M	T	W	T	F	S
		1	2	3	4	5
6	7	8	9	10	11	12
13	14	15	16	17	18	19
20	21	22	23	24	25	26
27	28	29	30			

PRAYER REQUESTS _____

_____

_____

_____

_____

APRIL 2014

❧ APRIL 2014 ❧

30 WEDNESDAY

"When she finds it, she calls her friends and neighbors together and says, 'Rejoice with me; I have found my lost coin.'" —Luke 15:9 (NIV)

MAY 1 THURSDAY

They go out to their work, searching for food.... —Job 24:5 (NKJV)

2 FRIDAY

He took up also the mantle of Elijah that fell from him, and went back, and stood by the bank of Jordan. —2 Kings 2:13 (KJV)

3 SATURDAY

Who hath despised the day of small things? —Zechariah 4:10 (KJV)

APRIL

GUIDEPOSTS DAILY PLANNER

But thank God for giving us the victory through our Savior Jesus Christ!
—1 CORINTHIANS 15:57 (TIB)

PRAYER FOR THE MONTH OF GROWING

A merry month, God?

Yes, but a serious one too.

Early spring's bornings are over,

And now we get down to the business

Of growth.

A good business, this.

A robin pulling a worm

For fledgling beaks.

The foal growing fat on mother's milk.

April's blossoms turning to fruit.

A magical business.

Your magic, God.

A LIVING PARABLE FOR MAY
FIND COURAGE
by Van Varner

Back in 1934, Thomas Carvel was a New Yorker without a job and almost no money. What he did have was a Model A Ford, a small house trailer, and a load of ice cream he'd made and hoped to sell.

On a Friday in summer, he headed for a picnic ground in the country, but a tire blew and Carvel found himself stranded at the roadside.

The owner of a pottery shop took pity on Carvel and helped him hook up his trailer, with the melting ice cream, to the shop's electricity. Carvel started selling his ice cream from that very spot. He learned the advantages of a stationary stand and, while puttering around the pottery shop, he found a device for dispensing soft ice cream, which became the foundation of one of America's largest ice-cream store chains.

"Welcome your bad breaks." "Turn lemons into lemonade." Call it any cliché you like, but defeat can be turned into victory. We know that because Jesus suffered the worst worldly defeat and gained the greatest victory in the history of the world.

MAY 2014 ❧

SUNDAY	MONDAY	TUESDAY	WEDNESDAY	THURSDAY	FRIDAY	SATURDAY
				1	2	3
4	5	6	7	8	9	10
11 MOTHER'S DAY	12	13	14	15	16	17
18	19	20	21	22	23	24
25	26 MEMORIAL DAY	27	28	29	30	31

NOTES

APRIL

S	M	T	W	T	F	S
		1	2	3	4	5
6	7	8	9	10	11	12
13	14	15	16	17	18	19
20	21	22	23	24	25	26
27	28	29	30			

JUNE

S	M	T	W	T	F	S
1	2	3	4	5	6	7
8	9	10	11	12	13	14
15	16	17	18	19	20	21
22	23	24	25	26	27	28
29	30					

GUIDEPOSTS DAILY PLANNER

OUR PRAYER: *Holy One, help me to live for*
Your kingdom this day, as wise children have modeled for me.

MAY

4
SUNDAY

And a little child shall lead them. —Isaiah 11:6 (AMP)

5
MONDAY

Fear ye not, stand still.... —Exodus 14:13 (KJV)

6
TUESDAY

Let every thing that hath breath praise the Lord. Praise ye the Lord. —Psalm 150:6 (KJV)

MAY

S	M	T	W	T	F	S
				1	2	3
4	5	6	7	8	9	10
11	12	13	14	15	16	17
18	19	20	21	22	23	24
25	26	27	28	29	30	31

PRAYER REQUESTS _____

_____

_____

_____

MAY 2014

❋ MAY 2014 ❋

7
WEDNESDAY

Follow God's example, therefore, as dearly loved children…. —Ephesians 5:1 (NIV)

8
THURSDAY

Give me relief from my distress; have mercy on me and hear my prayer. —Psalm 4:1 (NIV)

9
FRIDAY

"But when you are praying, first forgive anyone you are holding a grudge against…."
—Mark 11:25 (TLB)

10
SATURDAY

"Whoever belongs to God hears what God says…." —John 8:47 (NIV)

MAY

GUIDEPOSTS DAILY PLANNER

OUR PRAYER: *Dear God, give me the courage to put You and my family first this week so that I can tackle each day refreshed, rejuvenated, and ready to do Your work. Amen.*

MAY

11
SUNDAY
MOTHER'S DAY

For six days work is to be done, but the seventh day is a day of sabbath rest, holy to the Lord.... —Exodus 31:15 (NIV)

12
MONDAY

And if by grace, then it cannot be based on works; if it were, grace would no longer be grace. —Romans 11:6 (NIV)

13
TUESDAY

But I have called you friends.... —John 15:15 (RSV)

MAY

S	M	T	W	T	F	S
				1	2	3
4	5	6	7	8	9	10
11	12	13	14	15	16	17
18	19	20	21	22	23	24
25	26	27	28	29	30	31

PRAYER REQUESTS _____

_____

_____

_____

_____

MAY 2014

❀ MAY 2014 ❀

14
WEDNESDAY

And Jesus said to him, "If you can! All things are possible for one who believes."
—Mark 9:23 (ESV)

15
THURSDAY

"They are no longer two, but one flesh—and what God has joined together, let no one separate." —Matthew 19:6 (TIB)

16
FRIDAY

"Remain in me, as I also remain in you. No branch can bear fruit by itself; it must remain in the vine. Neither can you bear fruit unless you remain in me." —John 15:4 (NIV)

17
SATURDAY

I have much to write to you…so that our joy may be complete. —2 John 1:12 (NIV)

MAY

GUIDEPOSTS DAILY PLANNER

OUR PRAYER: *Thank You, God, for orchestrating Your mercies into my coincidences. Awaken me to Your gentle promptings that I might better share Your grace.*

18 SUNDAY

We may throw the dice, but the Lord determines how they fall. —Proverbs 16:33 (NLT)

19 MONDAY

I went down to the grove of nut trees to look at the new growth in the valley, to see if the vines had budded.... —Song of Songs 6:11 (NIV)

20 TUESDAY

"The one who had received the one talent went off and dug a hole in the ground and hid his master's money." —Matthew 25:18 (NRSV)

MAY

S	M	T	W	T	F	S
				1	2	3
4	5	6	7	8	9	10
11	12	13	14	15	16	17
18	19	20	21	22	23	24
25	26	27	28	29	30	31

PRAYER REQUESTS _____

MAY 2014

❧ MAY 2014 ❧

21 WEDNESDAY

"If you, then, though you are evil, know how to give good gifts to your children, how much more will your Father in heaven give good gifts to those who ask him!" —Matthew 7:11 (NIV)

22 THURSDAY

A soft answer turns away wrath, but harsh words cause quarrels. —Proverbs 15:1 (TLB)

23 FRIDAY

Let your eyes look directly ahead, and let your gaze be fixed straight in front of you... and all your ways will be established. —Proverbs 4: 25–26 (NAS)

24 SATURDAY

It was not you who sent me here, but God.... —Genesis 45:8 (RSV)

GUIDEPOSTS DAILY PLANNER

OUR PRAYER: *God, we thank You for illuminating our lives.*

MAY

25 SUNDAY

When Jesus spoke again to the people, he said, "I am the light of the world. Whoever follows me will never walk in darkness, but will have the light of life." —John 8:12 (NIV)

26 MONDAY

MEMORIAL DAY

"Go in peace, for we have sworn friendship with each other in the name of the Lord...." —1 Samuel 20:42 (NIV)

27 TUESDAY

I thank my God in all my remembrance of you, always offering prayer with joy in my every prayer for you all. —Philippians 1:3–4 (NAS)

MAY

S	M	T	W	T	F	S
				1	2	3
4	5	6	7	8	9	10
11	12	13	14	15	16	17
18	19	20	21	22	23	24
25	26	27	28	29	30	31

PRAYER REQUESTS

MAY 2014

❧ MAY 2014 ❧

28
WEDNESDAY

Grace to you and peace from God.... —Thessalonians 1:1 (RSV)

29
THURSDAY

Being confident of this, that he who began a good work in you will carry it on to completion until the day of Christ Jesus. —Philippians 1:6 (NIV)

30
FRIDAY

So the next generation would know them, even the children yet to be born, and they in turn would tell their children. —Psalm 78:6 (NIV)

31
SATURDAY

"They trusted in thee, and were not confounded." —Psalm 22:5 (KJV)

GUIDEPOSTS DAILY PLANNER

"You must love the Most High God with all your heart, with all your soul, with all your strength and with all your mind…." —LUKE 10:27 (TIB)

PRAYER FOR THE MONTH OF SHIMMERING NIGHTS

Creator, God, of all the sights of summer
None speaks the season more to me than
   the firefly,
A tiny lantern in the humid night,
Now brightening, now fading,
Beckoning to its mate with a slow wink
   of light.
Yet even as I hush
Before the mute magic of the lightning bug
I am reminded somehow of You,
For Your light is out there in the
   darkness too,
A silent beacon for those of faith to see,
Never dimming, but shining with
   constancy.

JUNE 2014

A LIVING PARABLE FOR JUNE
LOVE GOD by Van Varner

Many years ago, my prayers to God tended to resemble letters to Santa Claus—long lists of things I wanted God to do for me. Nowadays, however, I seldom close my eyes to pray that a simple little anecdote doesn't flash across my mind. It was one that actor Robert Young told.

He was listening to the bedtime prayers of one of his four daughters and she, like me, was going through her list of wants and "gimmees." But then she stopped, raised her head, opened her eyes to heaven and said, "And now, dear God, is there anything I can do for You?"

Ah, there it is again: the unvarnished faith of little children. And did I call that a "simple little anecdote?" It's not. That one tender question goes straight to the mark of what God expects of us children, big and little: to be mindful of God. After all, that was God's first—and greatest—commandment.

✤ JUNE 2014 ✤

SUNDAY	MONDAY	TUESDAY	WEDNESDAY	THURSDAY	FRIDAY	SATURDAY
1	2	3	4	5	6	7
8 PENTECOST	9	10	11	12	13	14 FLAG DAY
15 FATHER'S DAY	16	17	18	19	20	21 SUMMER BEGINS
22	23	24	25	26	27	28
29	30					

NOTES

MAY

S	M	T	W	T	F	S
				1	2	3
4	5	6	7	8	9	10
11	12	13	14	15	16	17
18	19	20	21	22	23	24
25	26	27	28	29	30	31

JULY

S	M	T	W	T	F	S
		1	2	3	4	5
6	7	8	9	10	11	12
13	14	15	16	17	18	19
20	21	22	23	24	25	26
27	28	29	30	31		

GUIDEPOSTS DAILY PLANNER

OUR PRAYER: *Thank You, God, for the gifts of Your communion table that keep us always in Your sight.*

JUNE

1 SUNDAY

This is my blood of the covenant, which is poured out for many for the forgiveness of sins. —Matthew 26:28 (NIV)

2 MONDAY

He sent a wind over the earth, and the waters receded. —Genesis 8:1 (NIV)

3 TUESDAY

The Lord is close to the brokenhearted and saves those who are crushed in spirit. —Psalm 34:18 (NIV)

JUNE

S	M	T	W	T	F	S
1	2	3	4	5	6	7
8	9	10	11	12	13	14
15	16	17	18	19	20	21
22	23	24	25	26	27	28
29	30					

PRAYER REQUESTS _____

_____

_____

_____

_____

JUNE 2014

❧ JUNE 2014 ❧

4
WEDNESDAY

"And when it reverts in the jubilee, the field shall be holy to the Lord, like a field set apart...." —Leviticus 27:21 (NAS)

5
THURSDAY

Therefore, as we have opportunity, let us do good to all people, especially to those who belong to the family of believers. —Galatians 6:10 (NIV)

6
FRIDAY

Now abideth faith, hope, charity, these three; but the greatest of these is charity. —1 Corinthians 13:13 (KJV)

7
SATURDAY

Therefore, if anyone is in Christ, he is a new creation; the old has gone, the new has come! —2 Corinthians 5:17 (NIV)

JUNE

GUIDEPOSTS DAILY PLANNER

OUR PRAYER: *Creator, help me stay focused as I work to stay on course and press on toward Your goals for me.*

8 SUNDAY

PENTECOST

I press toward the mark for the prize of the high calling of God.... —Philippians 3:14 (KJV)

9 MONDAY

Choose my instruction instead of silver, knowledge rather than choice gold. —Proverbs 8:10 (NIV)

10 TUESDAY

"Why did you bring us up out of Egypt to this terrible place?..." —Numbers 20:5 (NIV)

JUNE

JUNE

S	M	T	W	T	F	S
1	2	3	4	5	6	7
8	9	10	11	12	13	14
15	16	17	18	19	20	21
22	23	24	25	26	27	28
29	30					

PRAYER REQUESTS _____

_____

_____

_____

_____

JUNE 2014

❧ JUNE 2014 ❧

11
WEDNESDAY

"One thing I do know. I was blind but now I see!" —John 9:25 (NIV)

12
THURSDAY

"Therefore be merciful, just as your Father also is merciful." —Luke 6:36 (NKJV)

13
FRIDAY

"I create new heavens and a new earth...." —Isaiah 65:17 (RSV)

14
SATURDAY

FLAG DAY

Make a joyful noise unto the Lord.... —Psalm 98:4 (KJV)

GUIDEPOSTS DAILY PLANNER

OUR PRAYER: *God, You have given me family members who lived long, healthy lives. Help me to respect Your creation by doing my part to keep my body healthy.*

15
SUNDAY
FATHER'S DAY

"Behold, children are a heritage from the Lord..." —Psalm 127:3 (NKJV)

16
MONDAY

Teach us to number our days and recognize how few they are; help us to spend them as we should. —Psalm 90:12 (TLB)

17
TUESDAY

"Come to me, all you who are weary and burdened, and I will give you rest.... For my yoke is easy and my burden is light." —Matthew 11:28, 30 (NIV)

JUNE

JUNE

S	M	T	W	T	F	S
1	2	3	4	5	6	7
8	9	10	11	12	13	14
15	16	17	18	19	20	21
22	23	24	25	26	27	28
29	30					

PRAYER REQUESTS

JUNE 2014

❧ JUNE 2014 ❧

18 WEDNESDAY

"And what does the Lord require of you but...to walk humbly with your God?"
—Micah 6:8 (NRSV)

19 THURSDAY

It is pointless that you get up early and stay up late, eating the bread of hard labor, because God gives sleep to those he loves. —Psalm 127:2 (CEB)

20 FRIDAY

Sing to him a new song; play skillfully, and shout for joy. —Psalm 33:3 (NIV)

21 SATURDAY

SUMMER BEGINS

And she opened a bottle of milk.... —Judges 4:19 (KJV)

OUR PRAYER: *Lord, our relationships live because of Your compelling love.*

22
SUNDAY

For Christ's love compels us.... —2 Corinthians 5:14 (NIV)

23
MONDAY

This is the day which the Lord has made.... —Psalm 118:24 (RSV)

24
TUESDAY

Every good and perfect gift is from above.... —James 1:17 (NIV)

JUNE

JUNE

S	M	T	W	T	F	S
1	2	3	4	5	6	7
8	9	10	11	12	13	14
15	16	17	18	19	20	21
22	23	24	25	26	27	28
29	30					

PRAYER REQUESTS _____

JUNE 2014

It's time to order your copy of
Guideposts Daily Planner 2015!

3 EASY WAYS TO ORDER:

1. **Order by mail.** Return the coupon with payment.
2. **Phone.** Call (800) 932-2145.
3. **Order online** and **SAVE 10%** Visit ShopGuideposts.org/DP2015. Use promo code DP2015.

(RETURN PORTION OF THIS FORM WITH YOUR PAYMENT.)

ORDER BY MAIL. Pay with check.

Yes! Send me *Guideposts Daily Planner 2015* for just $14.95 plus shipping and processing.*

_____
Your Name (please print)

_____
Mailing Address

_____
City   State   ZIP

Total copies ordered _____   Amount Enclosed $ _____   14R74268FP

Method of Payment

*Connecticut/New York residents, please add sales tax.

Payment must accompany your order.

Please enclose your personal check or money order payable to Guideposts. No cash please.

Please allow 4 weeks for delivery.

Mail payment to:
Guideposts
PO Box 5815
Harlan, Iowa 51593

Guideposts

Guideposts

LOOKING FOR A GREAT GIFT IDEA?

Your search has ended! *Guideposts Daily Planner* makes a great gift that will be appreciated by everyone on your holiday list.

GUIDEPOSTS DAILY PLANNER OFFERS YOU ALL OF THIS AND MORE!

- Organization at a glance
- Moving devotions to mark the passing months
- Hidden spiral binding, so your planner will lay flat
- A special place for prayer requests
- Encouraging Scripture quotes to start each day

❖ JUNE 2014 ❖

25 WEDNESDAY

The Lord's lovingkindnesses indeed never cease.... —Lamentations 3:22 (NAS)

26 THURSDAY

Here is a list of some of the parts he has placed in his church, which is his body... Those who can help others.... —1 Corinthians 12:28 (TLB)

27 FRIDAY

"Blessed are you who weep now, for you will laugh." —Luke 6:21 (NRSV)

28 SATURDAY

He will cover you with his pinions, and under his wings you will find refuge.... —Psalm 91:4 (NRSV)

JUNE

GUIDEPOSTS DAILY PLANNER

And for anyone who is in Christ, there is a new creation. The old order has passed away; now everything is new! —2 CORINTHIANS 5:17 (TIB)

PRAYER FOR THE MONTH OF FIERY DAYS

God, as the kids indulge in castle construction
And the grown-ups lie baking in the sun,
I sit and look out to the sea
And have these deep, unsummer-like
    thoughts about eternity.
Those clouds   those puffs of white
    lazing in the distance—
They've roused this reverie,
For as I look from cloud to sea and back to
    cloud again
I think about water, an ocean full of water,
Where it came from and where it will go.
And suddenly I sense the wonder of Your plan
That sends the water down from sky to land
    to sea
And back again and back again endlessly.
This makes me think that if You're a god
who will not waste a single drop of rain,
How carefully You must hoard each simple
    human soul.

JULY 2014

A LIVING PARABLE FOR JULY
CHANGE by Van Varner

They called you Big Molly, didn't they? You were big, all right, and loud and rough. The meanest gal in town. A judge told me about your husband, Arthur, and how you'd divorced him and had him thrown into the workhouse for not sending money to support your little boy, Dickie.

You'd been an overhead crane operator—man's work to most people, child's play to you. Then you got sick and tried to contact Arthur, so he could look after Dickie while you were in the hospital. That was the beginning.

Dickie played on the swings in the Salvation Army's playground. Then Arthur started helping the army people, and when you came out of the hospital a captain cared for you. You were surprised at such unsolicited kindness. When you got better, you attended some of the army's meetings.

Do you remember the day we met? You and Arthur had remarried. I found you in a bright kitchen, making sandwiches and stuffing eggs for a picnic. You were still big, with great clumsy, gentle hands, but you were not the Big Molly I'd heard about. You were soft-spoken, almost timid.

Why the change?

You told me: "I found the Christ that was in me all along."

JULY 2014

SUNDAY	MONDAY	TUESDAY	WEDNESDAY	THURSDAY	FRIDAY	SATURDAY
		1	2	3	4 INDEPENDENCE DAY	5
6	7	8	9	10	11	12
13	14	15	16	17	18	19
20	21	22	23	24	25	26
27	28	29	30	31		

NOTES

JUNE

S	M	T	W	T	F	S
1	2	3	4	5	6	7
8	9	10	11	12	13	14
15	16	17	18	19	20	21
22	23	24	25	26	27	28
29	30					

AUGUST

S	M	T	W	T	F	S
					1	2
3	4	5	6	7	8	9
10	11	12	13	14	15	16
17	18	19	20	21	22	23
24/31	25	26	27	28	29	30

GUIDEPOSTS DAILY PLANNER

OUR PRAYER: *God, thank You for blessing me with friends who encourage me to get outside, so I can appreciate all You have created.*

JUNE
29
SUNDAY

The next morning he was up long before daybreak and went out alone into the wilderness to pray. —Mark 1:35 (TLB)

30
MONDAY

My times are in your hands.... —Psalm 31:15 (NIV)

JULY
1
TUESDAY

"And regardless of what else you put on, wear love. It's your basic, all-purpose garment...." —Colossians 3:14 (MSG)

JULY

JULY

S	M	T	W	T	F	S
		1	2	3	4	5
6	7	8	9	10	11	12
13	14	15	16	17	18	19
20	21	22	23	24	25	26
27	28	29	30	31		

PRAYER REQUESTS _____

JULY 2014

JULY 2014

2 WEDNESDAY

When my anxious thoughts multiply within me, Your consolations delight my soul. —Psalm 94:19 (NAS)

3 THURSDAY

If there is any excellence and if anything worthy of praise, dwell on these things. —Philippians 4:8 (NAS)

4 FRIDAY

INDEPENDENCE DAY

O give thanks unto the Lord, for he is good....And gathered them out of the lands, from the east, and from the west, from the north, and from the south. —Psalm 107:1, 3 (KJV)

5 SATURDAY

Light in a messenger's eyes brings joy to the heart.... —Proverbs 15:30 (NIV)

JULY

OUR PRAYER: *Dear God, thank You for giving our forefathers and foremothers the dream to live in freedom and unity, and for those who are constantly fighting for our right to keep it alive.*

6
SUNDAY
God blessed the seventh day and made it holy, because on it he rested from all the work of creating that he had done. —Genesis 2:3 (NIV)

7
MONDAY
The fruit of the Spirit is...kindness.... —Galatians 5:22 (NIV)

8
TUESDAY
"If you are offering your gift at the altar and there remember that your brother has something against you.... First go and be reconciled." —Matthew 5:23–24 (NIV)

JULY

JULY

S	M	T	W	T	F	S
		1	2	3	4	5
6	7	8	9	10	11	12
13	14	15	16	17	18	19
20	21	22	23	24	25	26
27	28	29	30	31		

PRAYER REQUESTS _____

JULY 2014

JULY 2014

9 WEDNESDAY

And he shall be unto thee a restorer of thy life, and a nourisher of thine old age....
—Ruth 4:15 (KJV)

10 THURSDAY

Start children off on the way they should go, and even when they are old they will not turn from it. —Proverbs 22:6 (NIV)

11 FRIDAY

You will...turn and comfort me. —Psalm 71:21 (CJB)

12 SATURDAY

For the trumpet will sound, the dead will be raised imperishable, and we will be changed.
—1 Corinthians 15:52 (NIV)

JULY

GUIDEPOSTS DAILY PLANNER

OUR PRAYER: *Keep the wind in my sails, God, and let me know where to turn to find the breeze.*

13 SUNDAY
And he said to them, "Follow me, and I will make you fishers of men." Immediately they left their nets and followed him. —Matthew 4:19-20 (RSV)

14 MONDAY
A glorious throne, exalted from the beginning, is the place of our sanctuary. —Jeremiah 17:12 (NIV)

15 TUESDAY
"Everyone assembled here will know that the Lord rescues his people, but not with sword and spear. This is the Lord's battle, and he will give you to us!" —1 Samuel 17:47 (NLT)

JULY

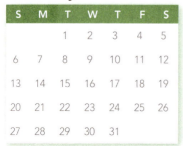

PRAYER REQUESTS

JULY 2014

✢ JULY 2014 ✢

16
WEDNESDAY

But Jacob was a peaceful man, living in tents. —Genesis 25:27 (NAS)

17
THURSDAY

"My grace is sufficient for you, for my power is made perfect in weakness".... —2 Corinthians 12:9 (NIV)"

18
FRIDAY

Our mouth was filled with laughter.... —Psalm 126:2 (RSV)

19
SATURDAY

Now to him who is able to do immeasurably more than all we ask or imagine.... —Ephesians 3:20 (NIV)

GUIDEPOSTS DAILY PLANNER

OUR PRAYER: *Remind me, God, of all those who have paid the price for following You.*

20
SUNDAY

Blessed are they which are persecuted for righteousness' sake…. —Matthew 5:10 (KJV)

21
MONDAY

Inasmuch as ye have done it unto one of the least of these my brethren, ye have done it unto me. —Matthew 25:40 (KJV)

22
TUESDAY

Commit to the Lord whatever you do, and your plans will succeed. —Proverbs 16:3 (NIV)

JULY

JULY

S	M	T	W	T	F	S
		1	2	3	4	5
6	7	8	9	10	11	12
13	14	15	16	17	18	19
20	21	22	23	24	25	26
27	28	29	30	31		

PRAYER REQUESTS _____

_____

_____

_____

_____

JULY 2014

☙ JULY 2014 ❧

23 WEDNESDAY
Return to Me with all your heart.... —Joel 2:12 (NAS)

24 THURSDAY
"But ask the animals, and they will teach you, or the birds in the sky, and they will tell you."
—Job 12:7 (NIV)

25 FRIDAY
For I will restore health unto thee, and I will heal thee of thy wounds, saith the Lord....
—Jeremiah 30:17 (KJV)

26 SATURDAY
"The kingdom of heaven is like treasure hidden in a field...." —Matthew 13:44 (NRSV)

JULY

OUR PRAYER: *Dear God, help me to know that if You need rest, I must rest too. Amen.*

27 SUNDAY

"He rested on the seventh day from all His work...Then God blessed the seventh day and sanctified it...." —Genesis 2:2-3 (NAS)

28 MONDAY

For I will leave in the midst of you a people humble and lowly.... —Zephaniah 3:12 (NRSV)

29 TUESDAY

Then the lame shall leap like a deer...For waters shall burst forth in the wilderness, and streams in the desert. —Isaiah 35:6 (NKJV)

JULY

S	M	T	W	T	F	S
		1	2	3	4	5
6	7	8	9	10	11	12
13	14	15	16	17	18	19
20	21	22	23	24	25	26
27	28	29	30	31		

PRAYER REQUESTS _____

_____

_____

_____

_____

JULY 2014

❧ JULY 2014 ❧

30
WEDNESDAY

Even the wilderness and desert will rejoice in those days, the desert will blossom with flowers. —Isaiah 35:1 (TLB)

31
THURSDAY

"For my thoughts are not your thoughts, neither are your ways my ways," declares the Lord. —Isaiah 55:8 (NIV)

AUvGUST

My comfort in my suffering is this: Your promise preserves my life. —Psalm 119:50 (NIV)

1
FRIDAY

2
SATURDAY

Don't jump to conclusions—there may be a perfectly good explanation for what you just saw. —Proverbs 25:8 (MSG)

JULY

GUIDEPOSTS DAILY PLANNER

There is no fear in love; but perfect love casteth out fear.... —1 JOHN 4:18 (KJV)

PRAYER FOR THE MONTH OF SHOOTING STARS

Dear God, three thousand years ago,
A shepherd boy who loved You
Counted his sheep at night
With the great stars blazing down.
Years later, as a mighty king, he wrote:
"The heavens declare the glory of God…"
So they do. That's why on August nights
I love to watch for shooting stars,
Those golden streaks of fire,
Tiny visitors from outer space,
Incandescent from the friction that they meet
When they invade our atmosphere.
God, let my passage through this world
Glow and sparkle sometimes so that those
   who watch
May say, "Ah, look. Did you see that?"
Meaning they have glimpsed a fragment of
   Your glory.

AUGUST 2014

A LIVING PARABLE FOR AUGUST
FACE FEAR by Van Varner

The writer Helen Worden Erskine was an animal lover, but she was afraid of crawling reptiles.

Years ago, on an assignment in what is now Pakistan, Mrs. Erskine had to stay in an old Karachi hotel where the service included a white-turbaned Muslim man-servant who slept on a mat outside her door. In the middle of the first night, she awakened suddenly. A large lizard with a green back and yellow belly was on the wall, watching her intently. "Help!" she screamed. "There's a lizard in my room!"

"Yes, madam," the man-servant replied, "there's a lizard in every room."

"I'm afraid of it. Kill it. Get rid of it."

"But, madam," he said, "if I remove the lizard, you will be plagued by all types of insects. Learn to live with your lizard. It is your friend. Once you realize this, your fear will vanish."

Thinking of St. Francis and his love for all living things, Mrs. Erskine vowed to accept that ugly little creature as a part of God's world as she herself was.

By the third night, Mrs. Erskine took a few grains of sugar from the dining room and gingerly offered them to the lizard. And by the time she left Karachi, she and the lizard were friends. She no longer feared it.

☙ AUGUST 2014 ☙

SUNDAY	MONDAY	TUESDAY	WEDNESDAY	THURSDAY	FRIDAY	SATURDAY
					1	2
3	4	5	6	7	8	9
10	11	12	13	14	15	16
17	18	19	20	21	22	23
24 / 31	25	26	27	28	29	30

NOTES

JULY

S	M	T	W	T	F	S
		1	2	3	4	5
6	7	8	9	10	11	12
13	14	15	16	17	18	19
20	21	22	23	24	25	26
27	28	29	30	31		

SEPTEMBER

S	M	T	W	T	F	S
	1	2	3	4	5	6
7	8	9	10	11	12	13
14	15	16	17	18	19	20
21	22	23	24	25	26	27
28	29	30				

GUIDEPOSTS DAILY PLANNER

OUR PRAYER: *Please help me trust You, God,*
rather than jumping to my own anxious conclusions.

3
SUNDAY

All discipline...seems not to be joyful, but sorrowful; yet...afterwards it yields the peaceful fruit of righteousness. —Hebrews 12:11 (NAS)

4
MONDAY

Remember how short my time is.... —Psalm 89:47 (KJV)

5
TUESDAY

I will always thank the Lord, I will never stop praising him. —Psalm 34:1 (GNB)

AUGUST

AUGUST

S	M	T	W	T	F	S
					1	2
3	4	5	6	7	8	9
10	11	12	13	14	15	16
17	18	19	20	21	22	23
24/31	25	26	27	28	29	30

PRAYER REQUESTS _____

_____

_____

_____

_____

AUGUST 2014

❧ AUGUST 2014 ❧

6 WEDNESDAY

A man that hath friends must shew himself friendly.... —Proverbs 18:24 (KJV)

7 THURSDAY

Religion that God...accepts as pure and faultless is this: to look after orphans and widows in their distress and to keep oneself from being polluted by the world. —James 1:27 (NIV)

8 FRIDAY

"When you come looking for me, you'll find me." —Jeremiah 29:13 (MSG)

9 SATURDAY

Steer clear of foolish discussions which lead people into the sin of anger with each other. —2 Timothy 2:16 (TLB)

AUGUST

GUIDEPOSTS DAILY PLANNER

OUR PRAYER: *Creator, teach me to embrace Your grace and forgiveness, for my need is great.*

10
SUNDAY

And Moses hid his face, for he was afraid to look at God. —Exodus 3:6 (NRSV)

11
MONDAY

My mouth will speak the praise of the Lord.... —Psalm 145:21 (NRSV)

12
TUESDAY

Then the Lord said to Moses, "I will rain down bread from heaven for you. The people are to go out each day and gather enough for that day...." —Exodus 16:4 (NIV)

AUGUST

AUGUST

S	M	T	W	T	F	S
					1	2
3	4	5	6	7	8	9
10	11	12	13	14	15	16
17	18	19	20	21	22	23
24/31	25	26	27	28	29	30

PRAYER REQUESTS _____

_____

_____

_____

_____

AUGUST 2014

✦ AUGUST 2014 ✦

13 WEDNESDAY
Now during these days he went out to the mountain to pray; and he spent the night in prayer to God. —Luke 6:12 (NRSV)

14 THURSDAY
For many years you were patient with them.... —Nehemiah 9:30 (NIV)

15 FRIDAY
If I speak in the tongues of men or of angels, but do not have love, I am only a resounding gong or a clanging cymbal. —1 Corinthians 13:1 (NIV)

16 SATURDAY
"A man's life does not consist in the abundance of his possessions." —Luke 12:15 (RSV)

AUGUST

GUIDEPOSTS DAILY PLANNER

OUR PRAYER: *Dear Jesus, thank You that anything I do in Your kingdom will have a lasting impact on people's lives. Open my eyes to the possibilities right outside my door today. Amen.*

17
SUNDAY

There are different kinds of service, but the same Lord. —1 Corinthians 12:5 (NIV)

18
MONDAY

And he said to them, "Go into all the world and proclaim the good news to the whole creation." —Mark 16:15 (NRSV)

19
TUESDAY

Then Philip opened his mouth, and . . . preached Jesus to him. —Acts 8:35 (NAS)

AUGUST

AUGUST

S	M	T	W	T	F	S
					1	2
3	4	5	6	7	8	9
10	11	12	13	14	15	16
17	18	19	20	21	22	23
24/31	25	26	27	28	29	30

PRAYER REQUESTS _____

AUGUST 2014

❈ AUGUST 2014 ❈

20 WEDNESDAY

Value others above yourselves, not looking to your own interests but each of you to the interests of the others. —Philippians 2:3-4 (NIV)

21 THURSDAY

The Lord said to Abram, "Go from your country and your kindred and your father's house to the land that I will show you." —Genesis 12:1 (NRSV)

22 FRIDAY

Consider it pure joy, my brothers and sisters, whenever you face trials of many kinds. —James 1:2 (NIV)

23 SATURDAY

"The Lord bless you and keep you; the Lord make his face shine on you and be gracious to you; the Lord turn his face toward you and give you peace." —Numbers 6:24–26 (NIV)

AUGUST

GUIDEPOSTS DAILY PLANNER

OUR PRAYER: *God, wherever I choose to be today, help me be fully there.*

24 SUNDAY

Let your eyes look straight ahead; fix your gaze directly before you. —Proverbs 4:25 (NIV)

25 MONDAY

"For if you forgive men their trespasses, your heavenly Father will also forgive you."
—Matthew 6:14 (NKJV)

26 TUESDAY

And he said, The things which are impossible with men are possible with God.
—Luke 18:27 (KJV)

AUGUST

AUGUST

S	M	T	W	T	F	S
					1	2
3	4	5	6	7	8	9
10	11	12	13	14	15	16
17	18	19	20	21	22	23
24/31	25	26	27	28	29	30

PRAYER REQUESTS _____

AUGUST 2014

❧ AUGUST 2014 ❧

27 WEDNESDAY

"Even to your old age...I will carry you...." —Isaiah 46:4 (NAS)

28 THURSDAY

The Lord is good, a strong hold in the day of trouble; and he knoweth them that trust in him. —Nahum 1:7 (KJV)

29 FRIDAY

Holy, holy, holy...the whole earth is full of his glory. —Isaiah 6:3 (KJV)

30 SATURDAY

But Mary treasured up all these things and pondered them in her heart. —Luke 2:19 (NIV)

AUGUST

GUIDEPOSTS DAILY PLANNER

*When our actions please the Almighty,
Yahweh brings even our enemies to the peace table.* —PROVERBS 16:7 (TIB)

PRAYER FOR THE MONTH OF TEMPESTS

O mighty God,
This is the month when You permit great storms
To sweep across the seas and strike the land.
I've seen the proud trees writhe and fall
And felt the battered beaches shudder
With the crash of frenzied waters,
It's comforting to think that You hold
These mighty forces in the hollow of Your hand;
Wild though they seem, they're still a part
Of Your eternal plan.
You are the god of storms, not just gentle
   zephyrs.
Keep me mindful when the winds of change
Blow through my life. When the storm
   clouds gather,
Let me hide beneath the shadow of Your wings
Until the tempest is no more.

SEPTEMBER 2014

A LIVING PARABLE FOR SEPTEMBER
PRACTICE KINDNESS
by Van Varner

Some people make the mistake of equating kindness with softness.

There is a story about an old man named Ling Toy who for twenty years had owned a restaurant in a neighborhood. One day a young man named Wong opened one across the street. Ling Toy was distressed and began to spread false stories about Mr. Wong—how his kitchen was dirty and how he was too young to know the real art of Chinese cuisine.

None of this seemed to disturb Wong. Whenever someone told him what Ling Toy had said, he would reply, "You must be mistaken. Ling Toy could not possibly have said that. From everything I know about him, he's much too fine a man."

Well, slowly Wong's good words filtered back to Ling Toy, who was dumbfounded. The old man walked across the street and introduced himself. It marked the beginning of a long friendship.

What was the wisdom that Wong put to use? In his kitchen, hanging over the door where he could see it every time he came under attack, was a placard: "The enemy is best defeated who is defeated with kindness."

SEPTEMBER 2014

SUNDAY	MONDAY	TUESDAY	WEDNESDAY	THURSDAY	FRIDAY	SATURDAY
	1 LABOR DAY	2	3	4	5	6
7	8	9	10	11	12	13
14	15	16	17	18	19	20
21	22	23 FALL BEGINS	24	25 ROSH HASHANAH	26	27
28	29	30				

NOTES

AUGUST

S	M	T	W	T	F	S
					1	2
3	4	5	6	7	8	9
10	11	12	13	14	15	16
17	18	19	20	21	22	23
24/31	25	26	27	28	29	30

OCTOBER

S	M	T	W	T	F	S
			1	2	3	4
5	6	7	8	9	10	11
12	13	14	15	16	17	18
19	20	21	22	23	24	25
26	27	28	29	30	31	

GUIDEPOSTS DAILY PLANNER

OUR PRAYER: *Thank You, God, for reminding me that it's You, not the appreciation of others, that I seek.*

31
SUNDAY

Though the Lord is exalted, he looks kindly on the lowly; though lofty, he sees them from afar. —Psalm 138:6 (NIV)

SEPTEMBER

1
MONDAY

LABOR DAY

"Observe my Sabbaths and have reverence for my sanctuary. I am the Lord." —Leviticus 26:2 (NIV)

2
TUESDAY

If God didn't hesitate to put everything on the line for us…is there anything else he wouldn't gladly and freely do for us? —Romans 8:32 (MSG)

SEPTEMBER

SEPTEMBER

S	M	T	W	T	F	S
	1	2	3	4	5	6
7	8	9	10	11	12	13
14	15	16	17	18	19	20
21	22	23	24	25	26	27
28	29	30				

PRAYER REQUESTS _____

SEPTEMBER 2014

❧ SEPTEMBER 2014 ❧

3
WEDNESDAY
My spirit abides among you; do not fear. —Haggai 2:5 (NRSV)

4
THURSDAY
Lord, make me to know...the measure of my days.... —Psalm 39:4 (KJV)

5
FRIDAY
For this child I prayed.... —1 Samuel 1:27 (KJV)

6
SATURDAY
The Lord is your keeper.... —Psalm 121:5 (NAS)

SEPTEMBER

GUIDEPOSTS DAILY PLANNER

OUR PRAYER: *God, thank You for the faith passed on to me by my faith community.*

7
SUNDAY

I am reminded of your sincere faith, which first lived in your grandmother Lois and in your mother Eunice and, I am persuaded, now lives in you also. —2 Timothy 1:5 (NIV)

8
MONDAY

"Martha, you are worried and troubled about many things. But one thing is needed, and Mary has chosen that good part, which will not be taken away from her." —Luke 10:41–42 (NKJV)

9
TUESDAY

When my spirit was overwhelmed within me, Then You knew my path…. —Psalm 142:3 (NKJV)

SEPTEMBER

SEPTEMBER

S	M	T	W	T	F	S
		1	2	3	4	5	6
7	8	9	10	11	12	13
14	15	16	17	18	19	20
21	22	23	24	25	26	27
28	29	30				

PRAYER REQUESTS _____

_____

_____

_____

_____

SEPTEMBER 2014

SEPTEMBER 2014

10 WEDNESDAY
Dear children, let us not love with words or speech but with actions and in truth. —1 John 3:18 (NIV)

11 THURSDAY
"For where two or three gather in my name, there am I with them." —Matthew 18:20 (NIV)

12 FRIDAY
Pray for each other so that you can live together whole and healed. —James 5:16 (MSG)

13 SATURDAY
My heart says of you, "Seek his face!" Your face, Lord, I will seek. —Psalm 27:8 (NIV)

GUIDEPOSTS DAILY PLANNER

OUR PRAYER: *Thank You, God, for giving us spiritual leaders and friends to light our way.*

14
SUNDAY

"I will rescue my flock...." —Ezekiel 34:10 (NIV)

15
MONDAY

All the days ordained for me were written in your book before one of them came to be. —Psalm 139:16 (NIV)

16
TUESDAY

Seekest thou great things for thyself? seek them not.... —Jeremiah 45:5 (KJV)

SEPTEMBER

SEPTEMBER

S	M	T	W	T	F	S
	1	2	3	4	5	6
7	8	9	10	11	12	13
14	15	16	17	18	19	20
21	22	23	24	25	26	27
28	29	30				

PRAYER REQUESTS _____

_____

_____

_____

_____

SEPTEMBER 2014

❧ SEPTEMBER 2014 ❧

17
WEDNESDAY

You shall not wrong or oppress a resident alien, for you were aliens in the land of Egypt.
—Exodus 22:21 (NRSV)

18
THURSDAY

You are the God who performs miracles.... —Psalm 77:14 (NIV)

19
FRIDAY

Let the morning bring me word of your unfailing love, for I have put my trust in you.
Show me the way I should go, for to you I entrust my life. —Psalm 143:8 (NIV)

20
SATURDAY

For the Lord will be at your side and will keep your foot from being snared.
—Proverbs 3:26 (NIV)

SEPTEMBER

GUIDEPOSTS DAILY PLANNER

OUR PRAYER: *Everything I have, God, really belongs to You.*
Help me to release it today with a heart full of joy.

21 SUNDAY

"Behold, I will do a new thing...." —Isaiah 43:19 (NKJV)

22 MONDAY

Whatever you ask the Father in my name, he may give it to you. —John 15:16 (RSV)

23 TUESDAY

FALL BEGINS

Be still, and know that I am God.... —Psalm 46:10 (KJV)

SEPTEMBER

SEPTEMBER

S	M	T	W	T	F	S
	1	2	3	4	5	6
7	8	9	10	11	12	13
14	15	16	17	18	19	20
21	22	23	24	25	26	27
28	29	30				

PRAYER REQUESTS _____

_____

_____

_____

_____

SEPTEMBER 2014

✦ SEPTEMBER 2014 ✦

24 WEDNESDAY

I trust in your unfailing love; my heart rejoices in your salvation. I will sing the Lord's praise, for he has been good to me. —Psalm 13:5-6 (NIV)

25 THURSDAY

ROSH HASHANAH

Your robes are all fragrant with myrrh and aloes and cassia. From ivory palaces stringed instruments make you glad. —Psalm 45:8 (ESV)

26 FRIDAY

But you—who are you to judge your neighbor?—James 4:12 (NIV)

SEPTEMBER

27 SATURDAY

Praise be to the God and Father of the Lord Jesus Christ, the Father of compassion and the God of all comfort. —2 Corinthians 1:3 (NIV)

GUIDEPOSTS DAILY PLANNER

Always praying in the Spirit, with all your prayers and petitions. Pray constantly and attentively for all God's holy people. —EPHESIANS 6:18 (TIB)

PRAYER FOR THE MONTH OF CRISPING LEAVES

God,
The picture I now see
Is of a newly antlered deer,
Head cocked, sniffing the wind.
For the clarity of autumn's air
Makes October the month of scents;
The austere tang of crisping leaves.
The thick pungence of woodsmoke,
The redolence of the last rose.
Smell.
A sense I often take for granted.
I take too much
Of what You give for granted, God.
Yet an autumn scent
Suspended in October's perfect air
Is unmistakably Yours.

A LIVING PARABLE FOR OCTOBER
PRAY by Van Varner

One of my most beloved friends is a pickpocket. Well, a former pickpocket. He spent thirty years at his "trade," including three terms in prison, before he met a widow who changed his life.

The widow had sensed good in this man, and she did the only thing within her power to turn him around: She prayed. Constantly. Without ceasing. Then his sister began praying for him too.

Well, my friend began to lose his touch. He'd place his fingers on a large roll of bills, and it would slip from his grip. He'd lift a wallet, and it would be empty. He'd hear a soft voice calling him to turn to look, spot the police before they spotted him, and walk away. It was as though some strange power were guiding him. So great was the potency of those women's prayers that they prayed him out of business!

In time, my friend turned his life over to God and has since spent his remaining years trying to make amends for his past. He is an old man now. The widow is dead. But he was there to help when she, in turn, needed him.

It's a bittersweet story, for it not only shows me the great and mysterious power of prayer, but the possibility of redemption for each and every one of us.

OCTOBER 2014

OCTOBER 2014

SUNDAY	MONDAY	TUESDAY	WEDNESDAY	THURSDAY	FRIDAY	SATURDAY
			1	2	3	4 YOM KIPPUR
5	6	7	8	9	10	11
12	13	14	15	16	17	18
19	20	21	22	23	24	25 UNITED NATIONS DAY
26	27	28	29	30	31 HALLOWEEN	

NOTES

SEPTEMBER

S	M	T	W	T	F	S
	1	2	3	4	5	6
7	8	9	10	11	12	13
14	15	16	17	18	19	20
21	22	23	24	25	26	27
28	29	30				

NOVEMBER

S	M	T	W	T	F	S
						1
2	3	4	5	6	7	8
9	10	11	12	13	14	15
16	17	18	19	20	21	22
23/30	24	25	26	27	28	29

GUIDEPOSTS DAILY PLANNER

OUR PRAYER: *I will follow You today, God.*

SEPTEMBER

28
SUNDAY

We are surrounded by such a great cloud of witnesses…. —Hebrews 12:1 (NIV)

29
MONDAY

The Lord watches over the strangers…. —Psalm 146:9 (NKJV)

30
TUESDAY

"Come with me by yourselves to a quiet place and get some rest." —Mark 6:31 (NIV)

OCTOBER

OCTOBER

S	M	T	W	T	F	S
			1	2	3	4
5	6	7	8	9	10	11
12	13	14	15	16	17	18
19	20	21	22	23	24	25
26	27	28	29	30	31	

PRAYER REQUESTS _____

_____

_____

_____

_____

OCTOBER 2014

✤ OCTOBER 2014 ✤

OCTOBER

1 WEDNESDAY

"See, darkness covers the earth and thick darkness is over the peoples, but the Lord rises upon you...." —Isaiah 60:2 (NIV)

2 THURSDAY

Whatever is true, whatever is noble, whatever is right, whatever is pure, whatever is lovely, whatever is admirable...think about such things. —Philippians 4:8 (NIV)

3 FRIDAY

"Sit in silence...." —Isaiah 47:5 (NIV)

4 SATURDAY

YOM KIPPUR

You made me; you created me. Now give me the sense to follow your commands. —Psalm 119:73 (NLT)

GUIDEPOSTS DAILY PLANNER

OUR PRAYER: *I will find the strength and courage, God, to live outright through You.*

5
SUNDAY

A wife of noble character...is worth far more than rubies. —Proverbs 31:10 (NIV)

6
MONDAY

May your fountain be blessed, and may you rejoice in the wife of your youth. —Proverbs 5:18 (NIV)

7
TUESDAY

Wait for the Lord; be strong, and let your heart take courage.... —Psalm 27:14 (ESV)

OCTOBER

OCTOBER

S	M	T	W	T	F	S
			1	2	3	4
5	6	7	8	9	10	11
12	13	14	15	16	17	18
19	20	21	22	23	24	25
26	27	28	29	30	31	

PRAYER REQUESTS _____

OCTOBER 2014

❧ OCTOBER 2014 ❧

8 WEDNESDAY

Harden not your heart.... —Psalm 95:8 (KJV)

9 THURSDAY

And all thy children shall be taught of the Lord; and great shall be the peace of thy children. —Isaiah 54:13 (KJV)

10 FRIDAY

Resist not evil: but whosoever shall smite thee on thy right cheek, turn to him the other also. —Matthew 5:39 (KJV)

11 SATURDAY

Seek the Lord while he may be found; call on him while he is near. —Isaiah 55:6 (NIV)

OCTOBER

OUR PRAYER: *God, You are the Master Musician. Touch the keys of our hearts and draw out a melody that will make the world around us rejoice to be alive.*

12
SUNDAY

The Lord blessed the latter part of Job's life more than the former part..... —Job 42:12 (NIV)

13
MONDAY

A good name is more desirable than great riches.... —Proverbs 22:1 (NIV)

14
TUESDAY

Do not be overcome by evil, but overcome evil with good. —Romans 12:21 (NIV)

OCTOBER

OCTOBER

S	M	T	W	T	F	S
			1	2	3	4
5	6	7	8	9	10	11
12	13	14	15	16	17	18
19	20	21	22	23	24	25
26	27	28	29	30	31	

PRAYER REQUESTS _____

_____

_____

_____

_____

OCTOBER 2014

☀ OCTOBER 2014 ☀

15
WEDNESDAY

He refreshes my soul. He guides me along the right paths for his name's sake.
—Psalm 23:3 (NIV)

16
THURSDAY

For freedom Christ has set us free.... —Galatians 5:1 (RSV)

17
FRIDAY

You shall live in booths for seven days...so that your generations may know that I made the people of Israel live in booths. —Leviticus 23:42-43 (NRSV)

OCTOBER

18
SATURDAY

My little children, these things I write to you, so that you may not sin. And if anyone sins, we have an Advocate with the Father, Jesus Christ the righteous. —1 John 2:1 (NKJV)

OUR PRAYER: *Dear Lord, You are not curbed and typecast! You speak in myriad ways. Teach me Your meanings, and may I keep seeking until I find Your will for me.*

19
SUNDAY

And ye shall seek me, and find me, when ye shall search for me with all your heart. —Jeremiah 29:13 (KJV)

20
MONDAY

Your path led through the sea, your way through the mighty waters, though your footprints were not seen. —Psalm 77:19 (NIV)

21
TUESDAY

That you may become blameless and harmless, children of God without fault in the midst of a crooked and perverse generation.... —Philippians 2:15 (NKJV)

OCTOBER

OCTOBER

S	M	T	W	T	F	S
			1	2	3	4
5	6	7	8	9	10	11
12	13	14	15	16	17	18
19	20	21	22	23	24	25
26	27	28	29	30	31	

PRAYER REQUESTS _____

OCTOBER 2014

❧ OCTOBER 2014 ❧

22 WEDNESDAY

"Whoever hears my word and believes him who sent me has eternal life and will not be judged but has crossed over from death to life." —John 5:24 (NIV)

23 THURSDAY

Then they sat on the ground with him for seven days and seven nights. No one said a word to him, because they saw how great his suffering was. —Job 2:13 (NIV)

24 FRIDAY

UNITED NATIONS DAY

We take captive every thought to make it obedient to Christ. —2 Corinthians 10:5 (NIV)

25 SATURDAY

Let us run with patience the particular race that God has set before us. —Hebrews 12:1 (TLB)

OCTOBER

OUR PRAYER: *God, thank You for giving me exactly what I need, when I need it the most.*

26 SUNDAY

You have searched me, Lord, and you know me. —Psalm 139:1 (NIV)

27 MONDAY

"But the seed on good soil stands for those with a noble and good heart, who hear the word, retain it, and by persevering produce a crop." —Luke 8:15: (NIV)

28 TUESDAY

Even though I walk through the darkest valley, I will fear no evil, for you are with me; your rod and your staff, they comfort me. —Psalm 23:4 (NIV)

OCTOBER

OCTOBER

S	M	T	W	T	F	S
			1	2	3	4
5	6	7	8	9	10	11
12	13	14	15	16	17	18
19	20	21	22	23	24	25
26	27	28	29	30	31	

PRAYER REQUESTS _____

_____

_____

_____

_____

OCTOBER 2014

❧ OCTOBER 2014 ❧

29
WEDNESDAY

May God's grace and blessing be upon all who sincerely love our Lord Jesus Christ. —Ephesians 6:24 (TLB)

30
THURSDAY

You will surely forget your trouble, recalling it only as waters gone by. Life will be brighter than noonday, and darkness will become like morning. —Job 11:16–17 (NIV)

31
FRIDAY

HALLOWEEN

One gives freely, yet grows all the richer.... —Proverbs 11:24 (ESV)

OCTOBER

NOVEMBER

The Lord will prepare a feast of rich food for all peoples, a banquet of aged wine.... —Isaiah 25:6 (NIV)

1
SATURDAY

ALL SAINTS DAY

GUIDEPOSTS DAILY PLANNER

A merry heart maketh a cheerful countenance.... —PROVERBS 15:13 (KJV)

PRAYER FOR THE MONTH OF WINTER THOUGHTS

God,
Now that we are in
The deeper reaches of autumn
And the wind is growling
Through the trees
And snatching the gold and copper leaves
From their branches,
I am beginning to have winter thoughts.
And I think
How I, too, should prepare
For harsher seasons
By getting down to basics,
By stripping myself
Of gaudy pretensions
And coming to You
Quietly
In all simplicity.

A LIVING PARABLE FOR NOVEMBER
LAUGH by Van Varner

I still remember a story that the late Harry Hershfield, one of America's most brilliant wits, told me. It was about a man who had become so discouraged with life that he bought a loaf of bread at a store, then went to a railroad crossing and stretched himself out across the tracks.

A police officer saw this bewildering sight and rushed up to him, asking, "What do you think you're doing?"

"Waiting for the train to run over me," the man replied.

"But why the loaf of bread?"

"The way the trains run here," the man answered, "you could starve to death while waiting for one."

Harry Hershfield didn't tell that story just to amuse me. He was making a point: That there is irony in our lives, and even in the darkest situation we can take ourselves too seriously. The greatest therapy in the world is the ability to get out of our own way long enough to observe ourselves—and sometimes even laugh at ourselves.

NOVEMBER 2014

SUNDAY	MONDAY	TUESDAY	WEDNESDAY	THURSDAY	FRIDAY	SATURDAY
						1 ALL SAINTS DAY
2 ALL SOULS DAY / DAYLIGHT SAVING TIME ENDS	3	4 ELECTION DAY	5	6	7	8
9	10	11 VETERANS DAY	12	13	14	15
16	17	18	19	20	21	22
23 1ST SUNDAY IN ADVENT 30	24 GUIDEPOSTS THANKSGIVING DAY OF PRAYER	25	26	27 THANKSGIVING	28	29

NOTES

OCTOBER

S	M	T	W	T	F	S
			1	2	3	4
5	6	7	8	9	10	11
12	13	14	15	16	17	18
19	20	21	22	23	24	25
26	27	28	29	30	31	

DECEMBER

S	M	T	W	T	F	S
	1	2	3	4	5	6
7	8	9	10	11	12	13
14	15	16	17	18	19	20
21	22	23	24	25	26	27
28	29	30	31			

GUIDEPOSTS DAILY PLANNER

OUR PRAYER: *God, I want a faith as big as Your generosity.*

2
SUNDAY
ALL SOULS DAY /
DAYLIGHT
SAVING TIME
ENDS

"For with the measure you use, it will be measured to you." —Luke 6:38 (NIV)

3
MONDAY

"As long as I am in the world, I am the light of the world." —John 9:5 (ESV)

4
TUESDAY
ELECTION DAY

To every thing there is a season, and a time to every purpose under the heaven:
A time to be born, and a time to die; a time to plant.... —Ecclesiastes 3:1–2 (KJV)

NOVEMBER

NOVEMBER

S	M	T	W	T	F	S
						1
2	3	4	5	6	7	8
9	10	11	12	13	14	15
16	17	18	19	20	21	22
23/30	24	25	26	27	28	29

PRAYER REQUESTS _____

NOVEMBER 2014

❧ NOVEMBER 2014 ❧

5
WEDNESDAY

"Peace I leave with you; my peace I give you. I do not give to you as the world gives. Do not let your hearts be troubled and do not be afraid." —John 14:27 (NIV)

6
THURSDAY

"I called you so often, but you wouldn't come. I reached out to you, but you paid no attention." —Proverbs 1:24 (NLT)

7
FRIDAY

For my thoughts are not your thoughts.... —Isaiah 55:8 (KJV)

8
SATURDAY

Having been firmly rooted and now being built up in Him.... —Colossians 2:7 (NAS)

NOVEMBER

GUIDEPOSTS DAILY PLANNER

OUR PRAYER: *God, let my work reflect Yours.*

9
SUNDAY

"If you love those who love you, what credit is that to you?..." —Luke 6:32 (NRSV)

10
MONDAY

"For where your treasure is, there your heart will be also." —Luke 12:34 (NKJV)

11
TUESDAY

VETERANS DAY

When you lie down, you will not be afraid; when you lie down, your sleep will be sweet.
—Proverbs 3:24 (NIV)

NOVEMBER

NOVEMBER

S	M	T	W	T	F	S
						1
2	3	4	5	6	7	8
9	10	11	12	13	14	15
16	17	18	19	20	21	22
23/30	24	25	26	27	28	29

PRAYER REQUESTS _____

_____

_____

_____

_____

NOVEMBER 2014

❧ NOVEMBER 2014 ❧

12
WEDNESDAY

By faith we understand that the universe was formed at God's command, so that what is seen was not made out of what was visible. —Hebrews 11:3 (NIV)

13
THURSDAY

When my soul fainted within me I remembered the Lord.... —Jonah 2:7 (KJV)

14
FRIDAY

And now, behold, we are in thine hand.... —Joshua 9:25 (KJV)

15
SATURDAY

Outdo one another in showing honor. —Romans 12:10 (ESV)

NOVEMBER

GUIDEPOSTS DAILY PLANNER

OUR PRAYER: *God, may I never be too timid to share my gifts or ask someone to share theirs.*

16
SUNDAY

Now there are varieties of gifts, but the same Spirit; and there are varieties of service, but the same Lord. —1 Corinthians 12:4-5 (RSV)

17
MONDAY

And I will say to them which were not my people, Thou art my people.... —Hosea 2:23 (KJV)

18
TUESDAY

"Greater love has no one than this: to lay down one's life for one's friends." —John 15:13 (NIV)

NOVEMBER

NOVEMBER

S	M	T	W	T	F	S
						1
2	3	4	5	6	7	8
9	10	11	12	13	14	15
16	17	18	19	20	21	22
23/30	24	25	26	27	28	29

PRAYER REQUESTS _____

_____

_____

_____

_____

NOVEMBER 2014

❧ NOVEMBER 2014 ❧

19 WEDNESDAY

I remember my affliction and my wandering….I well remember them, and my soul is downcast within me. —Lamentations 3:19–20 (NIV)

20 THURSDAY

"Your words were found, and I ate them, And Your word was to me the joy and rejoicing of my heart; For I am called by Your name, O Lord God of hosts." —Jeremiah 15:16 (NKJV)

21 FRIDAY

"Anyone who loves their life will lose it, while anyone who hates their life in this world will keep it for eternal life." —John 12:25 (NIV)

22 SATURDAY

Be of good cheer; I have overcome the world. —John 16:33 (KJV)

NOVEMBER

GUIDEPOSTS DAILY PLANNER

OUR PRAYER: *Dear God, give me comfort when I miss Your people.*
My heart belongs to You, and that's the important part.

23
SUNDAY

The Lord is nigh unto all them that call upon him, to all that call upon him in truth.
—Psalm 145:18 (KJV)

24
MONDAY

GUIDEPOSTS
THANKSGIVING
DAY OF PRAYER

The words of a gossip are like choice morsels; they go down to a man's inmost parts.
—Proverbs 18:8 (NIV)

25
TUESDAY

God saw everything that He had made, and indeed it was very good.... —Genesis 1:31 (NKJV)

NOVEMBER

NOVEMBER

S	M	T	W	T	F	S
						1
2	3	4	5	6	7	8
9	10	11	12	13	14	15
16	17	18	19	20	21	22
23/30	24	25	26	27	28	29

PRAYER REQUESTS _____

_____

_____

_____

_____

NOVEMBER 2014

❧ NOVEMBER 2014 ❧

26 WEDNESDAY

O, give thanks to the Lord.... —Psalm 105:1 (RSV)

27 THURSDAY

THANKSGIVING

Give thanks in all circumstances.... —1 Thessalonians 5:18 (NIV)

28 FRIDAY

My cup overflows. —Psalm 23:5 (RSV)

29 SATURDAY

I pray that the God of our Lord Jesus Christ, the Father of glory, may give you a spirit of wisdom and revelation.... —Ephesians 1:17 (NRSV)

NOVEMBER

GUIDEPOSTS DAILY PLANNER

Whatsoever ye shall ask in prayer, believing, ye shall receive. —MATTHEW 21:22 (KJV)

PRAYER FOR THE MONTH OF THE COMING OF IMMANUEL

God,
In a season of deadness,
When the earth is locked in cold
And the winds sweep through skeleton trees,
We cherish those deep greens and blood reds
Of fir and holly
Standing stark
Against the barrenness of earth
And the whiteness of snow,
Because
In the depth of their colors,
We are reminded
That You came to make it
A season of joy.

A LIVING PARABLE FOR DECEMBER
BELIEVE by Van Varner

Captain Eddie Rickenbacker, a flying hero of World War I, had a lifetime of reasons for believing in the power of prayer, but none was more dramatic than when his plane crashed. He and seven other men scrambled aboard a life raft, and there huddled day after searing day, night after shivering night. What rations they had gave out, and by the seventh day it was obvious that they would all soon die.

Now Rickenbacker always carried a pocket Bible and read aloud from Matthew 6: "*Therefore, take no thought, saying, What shall we eat? or, What shall we drink? or Wherewithal shall we be clothed?...for your heavenly Father knoweth that ye have need of all these things.*" Then he led the men in prayer.

No more than an hour later, a seagull flew out of the vast reaches of nowhere, circled overhead, then came down for a landing on the life raft. The men grabbed it. *Food!*

The next day the wind rose, the ocean swelled, and the clouds opened up and drenched the men with rain. *Water!*

On the twenty-first day, the men were rescued.

The truth hasn't changed: We continue discovering how our extremity becomes God's opportunity.

DECEMBER 2014

DECEMBER 2014

SUNDAY	MONDAY	TUESDAY	WEDNESDAY	THURSDAY	FRIDAY	SATURDAY
	1	2	3	4	5	6
7 2ND SUNDAY IN ADVENT	8	9	10	11	12	13
14 3RD SUNDAY IN ADVENT	15	16	17 HANUKKAH	18	19	20
21 4TH SUNDAY IN ADVENT / WINTER BEGINS	22	23	24 CHRISTMAS EVE	25 CHRISTMAS	26	27
28	29	30	31 NEW YEAR'S EVE			

NOTES

NOVEMBER

S	M	T	W	T	F	S
						1
2	3	4	5	6	7	8
9	10	11	12	13	14	15
16	17	18	19	20	21	22
23/30	24	25	26	27	28	29

JANUARY 2015

S	M	T	W	T	F	S
				1	2	3
4	5	6	7	8	9	10
11	12	13	14	15	16	17
18	19	20	21	22	23	24
25	26	27	28	29	30	31

GUIDEPOSTS DAILY PLANNER

OUR PRAYER: *Creator God, thank You for Your merciful love that ignores our faults and promises us delights beyond what we can imagine.*

30 SUNDAY
1ST SUNDAY IN ADVENT

"To you is born this day in the city of David a Savior, who is the Messiah, the Lord." —Luke 2:11 (NRSV)

DECEMBER
1 MONDAY

For the Lord God will help me…. —Isaiah 50:7 (KJV)

2 TUESDAY

Praise him, sun and moon; praise him, all you shining stars. —Psalm 148:3 (NIV)

DECEMBER

DECEMBER

S	M	T	W	T	F	S
	1	2	3	4	5	6
7	8	9	10	11	12	13
14	15	16	17	18	19	20
21	22	23	24	25	26	27
28	29	30	31			

PRAYER REQUESTS _____

DECEMBER 2014

❧ DECEMBER 2014 ❧

3
WEDNESDAY

We live by faith, not by sight. —2 Corinthians 5:7 (NIV)

4
THURSDAY

She gave birth to her firstborn, a son. She wrapped him in cloths and placed him in a manger, because there was no room for them in the inn. —Luke 2:7 (NIV)

5
FRIDAY

Prepare ye the way of the Lord.... —Mark 1:3 (KJV)

6
SATURDAY

Father, forgive them; for they know not what they do.... —Luke 23:34 (KJV)

DECEMBER

GUIDEPOSTS DAILY PLANNER

OUR PRAYER: *Baby Jesus, our Sabbath rest, on this day You slept.*
Thank You for coming to us and healing us with Your presence, with Your offers of rest.

7
SUNDAY

2ND SUNDAY
IN ADVENT

There remains, then, a Sabbath-rest for the people of God. —Hebrews 4:9 (NIV)

8
MONDAY

"The people are to go out each day and gather enough for that day…." —Exodus 16:4 (NIV)

9
TUESDAY

"And now, when shall I also provide for my own house?" —Genesis 30:30 (NKJV)

DECEMBER

DECEMBER

S	M	T	W	T	F	S
	1	2	3	4	5	6
7	8	9	10	11	12	13
14	15	16	17	18	19	20
21	22	23	24	25	26	27
28	29	30	31			

PRAYER REQUESTS _____

_____

_____

_____

_____

DECEMBER 2014

❧ DECEMBER 2014 ❧

10 WEDNESDAY
It is the gift of God. —Ecclesiastes 3:13 (KJV)

11 THURSDAY
Always keep on praying. No matter what happens, always be thankful, for this is God's will for you who belong to Christ Jesus. —1 Thessalonians 5:17-18 (TLB)

12 FRIDAY
"[Nothing] shall be able to separate us from the love of God, which is in Christ Jesus our Lord." —Romans 8: 39 (NKJV)

13 SATURDAY
He shall give thee the desires of thine heart. —Psalm 37:4 (KJV)

DECEMBER

GUIDEPOSTS DAILY PLANNER

OUR PRAYER: *Creator God, reclaim my self-obsession for Your good ends! This I pray in the name of Your Son, Who promised us Your power and love, despite our failings.*

14 SUNDAY

3RD SUNDAY IN ADVENT

We know that all things work together for good for those who love God, who are called according to his purpose. —Romans 8:28 **(NRSV)**

15 MONDAY

"I will lead the blind by ways they have not known, along unfamiliar paths I will guide them…." —Isaiah 42:16 **(NIV)**

16 TUESDAY

I'm singing my heart out to God—what a victory!… —Exodus 15:1 **(MSG)**

DECEMBER

DECEMBER

S	M	T	W	T	F	S
	1	2	3	4	5	6
7	8	9	10	11	12	13
14	15	16	17	18	19	20
21	22	23	24	25	26	27
28	29	30	31			

PRAYER REQUESTS _____

_____

_____

_____

_____

DECEMBER 2014

➤ DECEMBER 2014 ❧

17
WEDNESDAY

HANUKKAH

"I came that they might have life, and have it abundantly." —John 10:10 (NRSV)

18
THURSDAY

"The Lord is good to those whose hope is in him...." —Lamentations 3:25 (NIV)

19
FRIDAY

"I was a stranger and you welcomed me...sick and you visited me...."
—Matthew 25:35–36 (ESV)

20
SATURDAY

"Do not judge, so that you may not be judged." —Matthew 7:1 (NRSV)

DECEMBER

GUIDEPOSTS DAILY PLANNER

OUR PRAYER: *God, thank You for light and beauty and love. Thank You for the gift of Your Son.*

21 SUNDAY

4TH SUNDAY
IN ADVENT /
WINTER BEGINS

For God…made his light shine in our hearts to give us the light of the knowledge of God's glory displayed in the face of Christ. —2 Corinthians 4:6 **(NIV)**

22 MONDAY

I was glad when they said to me, "Let us go to the house of the Lord!" —Psalm 122:1 **(RSV)**

23 TUESDAY

For he satisfieth the longing soul. —Psalm 107:9 **(KJV)**

DECEMBER

DECEMBER

S	M	T	W	T	F	S
	1	2	3	4	5	6
7	8	9	10	11	12	13
14	15	16	17	18	19	20
21	22	23	24	25	26	27
28	29	30	31			

PRAYER REQUESTS _____

_____

_____

_____

_____

DECEMBER 2014

❧ DECEMBER 2014 ❧

24
WEDNESDAY

CHRISTMAS
EVE

On entering the house, they saw the child with Mary his mother; and they knelt down and paid him homage.... —Matthew 2:11 (NRSV)

25
THURSDAY

CHRISTMAS

Jesus answered, "The work of God is this: to believe in the one he has sent." —John 6:29 (NIV)

26
FRIDAY

For He shall give His angels charge over you, to keep you in all your ways. —Psalm 91:11 (NKJV)

27
SATURDAY

Go to the ant, O sluggard; consider her ways, and be wise.... She prepares her food in summer, and gathers her sustenance in harvest. —Proverbs 6:6, 8 (RSV)

DECEMBER

GUIDEPOSTS DAILY PLANNER

OUR PRAYER: *God, help me to live in a spirit of hope each day of the year.*

28
SUNDAY

For I live in eager expectation and hope.... —Philippians 1:20 (TLB)

29
MONDAY

So teach us to number our days, That we may present to You a heart of wisdom. —Psalm 90:12 (NAS)

30
TUESDAY

I go to prepare a place for you. —John 14:2 (KJV)

DECEMBER

DECEMBER

S	M	T	W	T	F	S
	1	2	3	4	5	6
7	8	9	10	11	12	13
14	15	16	17	18	19	20
21	22	23	24	25	26	27
28	29	30	31			

PRAYER REQUESTS _____

_____

_____

_____

_____

DECEMBER 2014

➤ DECEMBER 2014 ➤

31
WEDNESDAY

NEW YEAR'S
EVE

"For the revelation awaits an appointed time; it speaks of the end and will not prove false. Though it linger, wait for it; it will certainly come and will not delay." —Habakkuk 2:3 (NIV)

JANUARY
2015

I am growing and becoming strong in spirit, filled with wisdom, and the grace of God is upon me. —Luke 2:40 (KJV)

1
THURSDAY

NEW YEAR'S
DAY

2
FRIDAY

"The Lord will fight for you; you need only be still." –Exodus 14:14 (NIV)

3
SATURDAY

"Be faithful until death, and I will give you the crown of life." –Revelation 2:10 (NAS)

DECEMBER

GUIDEPOSTS DAILY PLANNER

JANUARY 2015

SUNDAY	MONDAY	TUESDAY	WEDNESDAY	THURSDAY	FRIDAY	SATURDAY
				1 NEW YEAR'S DAY	2	3
4	5	6	7	8	9	10
11	12	13	14	15	16	17
18	19 MARTIN LUTHER KING JR. DAY	20	21	22	23	24
25	26	27	28	29	30	31

FEBRUARY 2015

SUNDAY	MONDAY	TUESDAY	WEDNESDAY	THURSDAY	FRIDAY	SATURDAY
1	2	3	4	5	6	7
8	9	10	11	12 ABRAHAM LINCOLN'S BIRTHDAY	13	14 VALENTINE'S DAY
15	16 PRESIDENTS' DAY	17	18 ASH WEDNESDAY	19	20	21
22 GEORGE WASHINGTON'S BIRTHDAY	23	24	25	26	27	28

MARCH 2015

SUNDAY	MONDAY	TUESDAY	WEDNESDAY	THURSDAY	FRIDAY	SATURDAY
1	2	3	4	5	6	7
8 DAYLIGHT SAVING TIME BEGINS	9	10	11	12	13	14
15	16	17 ST. PATRICK'S DAY	18	19	20 SPRING BEGINS	21
22	23	24	25	26	27	28
29 PALM SUNDAY	30	31				

APRIL 2015

SUNDAY	MONDAY	TUESDAY	WEDNESDAY	THURSDAY	FRIDAY	SATURDAY
			1	2 MAUNDY THURSDAY	3 PASSOVER / GOOD FRIDAY	4
5 EASTER	6	7	8	9	10	11
12	13	14	15	16	17	18
19	20	21	22 EARTH DAY	23	24	25
26	27	28	29	30		

2015 CALENDAR

JANUARY
S	M	T	W	T	F	S
				1	2	3
4	5	6	7	8	9	10
11	12	13	14	15	16	17
18	19	20	21	22	23	24
25	26	27	28	29	30	31

FEBRUARY
S	M	T	W	T	F	S
1	2	3	4	5	6	7
8	9	10	11	12	13	14
15	16	17	18	19	20	21
22	23	24	25	26	27	28

MARCH
S	M	T	W	T	F	S
1	2	3	4	5	6	7
8	9	10	11	12	13	14
15	16	17	18	19	20	21
22	23	24	25	26	27	28
29	30	31				

APRIL
S	M	T	W	T	F	S
			1	2	3	4
5	6	7	8	9	10	11
12	13	14	15	16	17	18
19	20	21	22	23	24	25
26	27	28	29	30		

MAY
S	M	T	W	T	F	S
					1	2
3	4	5	6	7	8	9
10	11	12	13	14	15	16
17	18	19	20	21	22	23
24/31	25	26	27	28	29	30

JUNE
S	M	T	W	T	F	S
	1	2	3	4	5	6
7	8	9	10	11	12	13
14	15	16	17	18	19	20
21	22	23	24	25	26	27
28	29	30				

JULY
S	M	T	W	T	F	S
			1	2	3	4
5	6	7	8	9	10	11
12	13	14	15	16	17	18
19	20	21	22	23	24	25
26	27	28	29	30	31	

AUGUST
S	M	T	W	T	F	S
						1
2	3	4	5	6	7	8
9	10	11	12	13	14	15
16	17	18	19	20	21	22
23/30	24/31	25	26	27	28	29

SEPTEMBER
S	M	T	W	T	F	S
		1	2	3	4	5
6	7	8	9	10	11	12
13	14	15	16	17	18	19
20	21	22	23	24	25	26
27	28	29	30			

OCTOBER
S	M	T	W	T	F	S
				1	2	3
4	5	6	7	8	9	10
11	12	13	14	15	16	17
18	19	20	21	22	23	24
25	26	27	28	29	30	31

NOVEMBER
S	M	T	W	T	F	S
1	2	3	4	5	6	7
8	9	10	11	12	13	14
15	16	17	18	19	20	21
22	23	24	25	26	27	28
29	30					

DECEMBER
S	M	T	W	T	F	S
		1	2	3	4	5
6	7	8	9	10	11	12
13	14	15	16	17	18	19
20	21	22	23	24	25	26
27	28	29	30	31		

2016 CALENDAR

JANUARY
S	M	T	W	T	F	S
					1	2
3	4	5	6	7	8	9
10	11	12	13	14	15	16
17	18	19	20	21	22	23
24/31	25	26	27	28	29	30

FEBRUARY
S	M	T	W	T	F	S
	1	2	3	4	5	6
7	8	9	10	11	12	13
14	15	16	17	18	19	20
21	22	23	24	25	26	27
28	29					

MARCH
S	M	T	W	T	F	S
		1	2	3	4	5
6	7	8	9	10	11	12
13	14	15	16	17	18	19
20	21	22	23	24	25	26
27	28	29	30	31		

APRIL
S	M	T	W	T	F	S
					1	2
3	4	5	6	7	8	9
10	11	12	13	14	15	16
17	18	19	20	21	22	23
24	25	26	27	28	29	30

MAY
S	M	T	W	T	F	S
1	2	3	4	5	6	7
8	9	10	11	12	13	14
15	16	17	18	19	20	21
22	23	24	25	26	27	28
29	30	31				

JUNE
S	M	T	W	T	F	S
			1	2	3	4
5	6	7	8	9	10	11
12	13	14	15	16	17	18
19	20	21	22	23	24	25
26	27	28	29	30		

JULY
S	M	T	W	T	F	S
					1	2
3	4	5	6	7	8	9
10	11	12	13	14	15	16
17	18	19	20	21	22	23
24/31	25	26	27	28	29	30

AUGUST
S	M	T	W	T	F	S
	1	2	3	4	5	6
7	8	9	10	11	12	13
14	15	16	17	18	19	20
21	22	23	24	25	26	27
28	29	30	31			

SEPTEMBER
S	M	T	W	T	F	S
				1	2	3
4	5	6	7	8	9	10
11	12	13	14	15	16	17
18	19	20	21	22	23	24
25	26	27	28	29	30	

OCTOBER
S	M	T	W	T	F	S
						1
2	3	4	5	6	7	8
9	10	11	12	13	14	15
16	17	18	19	20	21	22
23/30	24/31	25	26	27	28	29

NOVEMBER
S	M	T	W	T	F	S
		1	2	3	4	5
6	7	8	9	10	11	12
13	14	15	16	17	18	19
20	21	22	23	24	25	26
27	28	29	30			

DECEMBER
S	M	T	W	T	F	S
				1	2	3
4	5	6	7	8	9	10
11	12	13	14	15	16	17
18	19	20	21	22	23	24
25	26	27	28	29	30	31

❧ ANNIVERSARY GIFTS ❦

	TRADITIONAL	MODERN
1st	Paper	Clocks
2nd	Cotton	China
3rd	Leather	Crystal, glass
4th	Linen, silk	Appliances
5th	Wood	Silverware
6th	Iron	Wood objects
7th	Wool, copper	Desk sets
8th	Bronze	Linens, lace
9th	Pottery, china	Leather goods
10th	Tin, aluminum	Diamond
11th	Steel	Fashion jewelry
12th	Silk	Pearls, colored gems
13th	Lace	Textiles, furs
14th	Ivory	Gold jewelry
15th	Crystal	Watches
16th		Silver holloware
17th		Furniture
18th		Porcelain
19th		Bronze
20th	China	Platinum
21st		Brass, nickel
22nd		Copper
23rd		Silver plate
24th		Musical instruments
25th	Silver	Sterling silver
26th		Original pictures
27th		Sculpture
28th		Orchids
29th		New furniture
30th	Pearl	Diamond
31st		Timepieces
32nd		Conveyances (e.g., automobiles)
33rd		Amethyst
34th		Opal
35th	Coral (jade)	Jade
36th		Bone china

	TRADITIONAL	MODERN
37th		Alabaster
38th		Beryl, tourmaline
39th		Lace
40th	Ruby	Ruby
41st		Land
42nd		Improved real estate
43rd		Travel
44th		Groceries
45th	Sapphire	Sapphire
46th		Original poetry tribute
47th		Books
48th		Optical goods (e.g., telescope, microscope)
49th		Luxuries
50th	Gold	Gold
55th	Emerald	Emerald
60th	Diamond	Diamond
75th	Diamonds, diamondlike stones, gold	Diamonds, diamondlike stones, gold

❧ BIRTHSTONES & FLOWERS ❦

MONTH	STONE	FLOWER
January	Garnet	Carnation
February	Amethyst	Violet
March	Aquamarine	Daffodil
April	Diamond or White Topaz	Daisy
May	Emerald	Lily of the Valley
June	Pearl or Moonstone	Rose
July	Ruby	Larkspur
August	Peridot	Gladiolus
September	Sapphire	Aster
October	Opal	Calendula
November	Citrine	Chrysanthemum
December	Blue Topaz	Holly or Poinsettia

✦ BIRTHDAYS ✦

JANUARY

FEBRUARY

MARCH

APRIL

MAY

JUNE

JULY

AUGUST

SEPTEMBER

OCTOBER

NOVEMBER

DECEMBER

❧ NAMES & NUMBERS ❧

NAME	ADDRESS	TELEPHONE

NAME	ADDRESS	TELEPHONE

✦ A NOTE FROM THE EDITORS ✦

Guideposts Daily Planner is created each year by the Books and Inspirational Media Division of Guideposts, a nonprofit organization that touches millions of lives every day through products and services that inspire, encourage, help you grow in your faith, and celebrate God's love.

Your purchase of *Guideposts Daily Planner 2014* makes a difference. When you buy Guideposts products, you're helping fund our many outreach programs to military personnel, prisons, hospitals, nursing homes and educational institutions. If you'd like to be part of Guideposts' ministries by making a contribution, please visit GuidepostsFoundation.org to find out more about ways you can help.

You can order the 2015 edition of *Guideposts Daily Planner* anytime after July 2014. To order, visit ShopGuideposts.org, call (800) 932-2145 or write Guideposts, PO Box 5815, Harlan, Iowa 51593.